SCHOLAST
ENGLISH SKI

Comprehension
Year 4

TERMS AND CONDITIONS

IMPORTANT – PERMITTED USE AND WARNINGS – READ CAREFULLY BEFORE USING

Copyright in the software contained in this CD-ROM and in its accompanying material belongs to Scholastic Limited. All rights reserved. © 2009, 2016 Scholastic Ltd.

Save for these purposes, or as expressly authorised in the accompanying materials, the software may not be copied, reproduced, used, sold, licensed, transferred, exchanged, hired, or exported in whole or in part or in any manner or form without the prior written consent of Scholastic Ltd. Any such unauthorised use or activities are prohibited and may give rise to civil liabilities and criminal prosecutions.

The material contained on this CD-ROM may only be used in the context for which it was intended in *Scholastic English Skills*, and is for use only in the school which has purchased the book and CD-ROM, or by the teacher who has purchased the book and CD-ROM. Permission to download images is given for purchasers only and not for users from any lending service. Any further use of the material contravenes Scholastic Ltd's copyright and that of other rights holders.

This CD-ROM has been tested for viruses at all stages of its production. However, we recommend that you run virus-checking software on your computer systems at all times. Scholastic Ltd cannot accept any responsibility for any loss, disruption or damage to your data or your computer system that may occur as a result of using either the CD-ROM or the data held on it.

IF YOU ACCEPT THE ABOVE CONDITIONS YOU MAY PROCEED TO USE THE CD-ROM.

Recommended system requirements:

Windows: XP (Service Pack 3), Vista (Service Pack 2), Windows 7 or Windows 8 with 2.33GHz processor
Mac: OS 10.6 to 10.8 with Intel Core™ Duo processor
1GB RAM (recommended)
1024 x 768 Screen resolution
CD-ROM drive (24x speed recommended)
Adobe Reader (version 9 recommended for Mac users)
Broadband internet connections (for installation and updates)

For all technical support queries (including no CD drive), please phone Scholastic Customer Services on 0845 6039091.

Authors
Donna Thomson and
Elspeth Graham

Editor
Rachel Morgan

Assistant editors
Marion Archer, Alex Albrighton and
Suzanne Adams

CD-ROM design and development team
Hannah Barnett, Phil Crothers and
MWA Technologies Private Ltd

Series designers
Shelley Best and Anna Oliwa

Book layout
Quadrum Solutions Ltd

Illustrations
Robin Edmonds/Beehive Illustration

The rights of Donna Thomson and Elspeth Graham to be identified as the authors of this work has been asserted by them in accordance with the Copyright, Designs and Patents Act 1988.

All rights reserved. This book is sold subject to the condition that it shall not, by way of trade or otherwise, be lent, hired out or otherwise circulated without the publisher's prior consent in any form of binding or cover other than that in which it is published and without a similar condition, including this condition, being imposed upon the subsequent purchaser.

No part of this publication may be reproduced, stored in a retrieval system, or transmitted, in any form or by any means, electronic, mechanical, photocopying, recording or otherwise, other than for the purposes described in the lessons in this book, without the prior permission of the publisher. This book remains copyright, although permission is granted to copy pages where indicated for classroom distribution and use only in the school which has purchased the book, or by the teacher who has purchased the book, and in accordance with the CLA licensing agreement. Photocopying permission is given only for purchasers and not for borrowers of books from any lending service.

Extracts from The National Curriculum for England, English Programme of Study © Crown Copyright. Reproduced under the terms of the Open Government Licence (OGL). www.nationalarchives.gov.uk/doc/open-government-licence/version/3/

Scholastic Education, an imprint of Scholastic Ltd
Book End, Range Road, Witney, Oxfordshire, OX29 0YD
Registered office: Westfield Road, Southam,
Warwickshire CV47 0RA
www.scholastic.co.uk

Printed and bound by Ashford Colour Press
Text © 2009, 2016 Donna Thomson
© 2009, 2016 Scholastic Ltd
1 2 3 4 5 6 7 8 9   6 7 8 9 0 1 2 3 4 5

British Library Cataloguing-in-Publication Data
A catalogue record for this book is available from the British Library.
ISBN 978-1407-14175-6

Acknowledgements

The publishers gratefully acknowledge permission to reproduce the following copyright material: **Andersen Press Ltd** for the use of text and an illustration from *Flabby Cat and Slobby Dog* by Jeanne Willis and Tony Ross. Text © 2010, Jeanne Willis. Illustration © 2010, Tony Ross. (2010, Andersen Press Ltd); text and illustrations from *Fred* by Posy Simmonds. Text and illustrations © 1987, Posy Simmonds. (1987, Jonathan Cape); text and an illustration from *Dr Xargle's Book of Earth Tiggers* by Jeanne Willis and Tony Ross. Text © 1990, Jeanne Willis. Illustration © 1990, Tony Ross. (1990, Andersen Press Ltd). **A.P. Watt** for the use of a text extract from *I Love Guinea Pigs* by Dick King-Smith. Text © 1994, Foxbusters Ltd. (1994, Walker Books Ltd). **Artist Partners Ltd** on behalf of David Roberts for the use of an illustration from *Rapunzel* by Lynn and David Roberts. Illustration © 2003, David Roberts. (2003, Chrysalis Children's Books). **Catnip Publishing Ltd** for the use of text and an illustration from *The War and Freddy* by Dennis Hamley and George Buchanan. Text © 1991, Dennis Hamley. Illustration © 1991, George Buchanan. (2007, Catnip Publishing Ltd). **David Higham Associates** for the use of a text extract from *Billy the Kid* by Michael Morpurgo. Text © 2000, Michael Morpurgo. (2000, Pavilion Books Ltd). **Egmont UK Ltd** for the use of the cover image from *The Three Little Wolves and the Big Bad Pig* by Eugene Trivizas and Helen Oxenbury. Text © 1993, Eugene Trivizas. Illustration © 1993, Helen Oxenbury. (1993, Egmont Books Ltd). **Michael Foreman** for the use of an illustration from *Billy the Kid* by Michael Morpurgo. Illustration © 2000, Michael Foreman. (2000, Pavilion Books Ltd). **Frances Lincoln Ltd** for the use of text and an illustration from *The Dragon Snatcher* by M.P. Robertson. Text and illustrations © 2005, M.P. Robertson. (2005, Frances Lincoln Children's Books). **Elspeth Graham** on behalf of Mal Peet for the use of the poem 'Seed' from *Rainbows, Roots and Magic Shoots* compiled by Mal Peet and Elspeth Graham. Poem © 2002, Mal Peet. (2002, Oxford University Press). **Nigel Gray** for the use of the poem 'My Cat' from *Another First Book of Poetry* compiled by John Foster. Poem © 1975, Nigel Gray. (1987, Oxford University Press). **Pavilion Children's Books** for the use of text and an illustration from *Tales from the African Plains* by Anne Gatti. Text © 1994, Pavilion Books. Illustrations © 1994, Gregory Alexander. (1994, Pavilion Books Ltd). **Penguin Books Ltd** for the use of a text and illustration extract from *Beware of Girls* by Tony Blundell. © 2002, Tony Blundell. (2002, Puffin Books); text and illustrations from *Beware of Boys* by Tony Blundell. © 1993, Tony Blundell. (1993, Puffin Books). **Random House Children's Books** for the use of two pages from *Toys in Space* by Mini Grey. © 2012, Mini Grey. (2012, Jonathan Cape); a text and illustration extract from *The Sea Monster* by Chris Wormell. © 2005, Chris Wormell. (2005, Jonathan Cape) . **Lynn Roberts** for the use of a text extract from *Rapunzel* by Lynn and David Roberts. Text © 2003, Lynn Roberts. (2003, Chrysalis Children's Books). **Walker Books Ltd** for the use of text and an illustration from *Jonathan Swift's Gulliver* by Martin Jenkins, illustrated by Chris Riddell. Text © 2004 Martin Jenkins. Illustrations © 2004 Chris Riddell. (2004, Walker Books Ltd); text and illustrations from *The Children who Smelled a Rat* by Allan Ahlberg, illustrated by Katharine McEwen. Text © 2005, Allan Ahlberg. Illustrations © 2005, Katharine McEwen. (2005, Walker Books Ltd); text and illustration extract from *I love Guinea Pigs* by Dick King Smith. Text © 1994, Foxbusters Ltd. Illustrations © 1994, Anita Jeram. (1994, Walker Books Ltd); text and illustrations from *Hansel and Gretel* by Jane Ray. © 1997, Jane Ray. (1997, Walker Books Ltd). Every effort has been made to trace copyright holders for the works reproduced in this book, and the publishers apologise for any inadvertent omissions.

Contents

Chapter 1
Retelling

Chapter 2
Literal questioning

Chapter 3
Prediction

Chapter 4
Inference

Chapter 5
Clarification

Chapter 6
Evaluation

Chapter 7
Review

Introduction

The Scholastic English Skills: Comprehension

Comprehension is the ability to understand and elicit meaning from any type of written or illustrated material. It is the reason for reading. If readers can read the words but do not understand what they mean, they are not really reading.

This series offers teachers carefully structured guidance on how to use the essential comprehension skills of summarising, predicting, clarifying and questioning to extract the author's meaning. Each book is progressive and supports the teaching and development of these comprehension strategies. The series also offers teachers a generic framework for teaching reciprocal reading – a process that provides children with the confidence to explore and enjoy a range of 'real' books beyond the samples featured in the series. The skills pages show the children how to gather information, respond to questions meaningfully and generate their own literal, inferential and evaluative questions from quality fiction and non-fiction extracts. It also provides comprehension assessment materials.

Overview of the teaching of comprehension

To fully engage children in the reading process and help them to explore and make sense of a range of texts, they need to understand the skills involved in how we make meaning. Alongside summarising, clarifying and predicting, they need to be able to identify and apply the three fundamental questioning skills:

- Literal – explicit meaning. (Who? What? Where?)
- Inference – hidden and implied meaning. (Detective work – thinking and searching for clues to make deductions. Why? How do you know that?)
- Evaluation – personal meaning. (Using own experience to explain events or characters' actions, feelings and behaviour and linking them to the author's viewpoint. Why do you think…?)

These skills enable children to have full understanding of information, whether it is presented through text or pictures, and are central to bringing meaning and reasoning to learning to read and learning in general.

Comprehension is not something that happens after reading. Good readers use their experience and knowledge of the world, alongside their knowledge of vocabulary and language structure, to make sense of the text and relate to the author's viewpoint. Good readers monitor their understanding as they read and know how to resolve their difficulties with comprehension as the problems arise.

About the product

This book contains seven chapters. Each chapter focuses on a different aspect of comprehension, and is organised into four sections with clear objectives, background information, teaching ideas and photocopiable pages for use in whole-class teaching, with groups or for independent work. Each chapter also features a poster.

Posters

Each chapter has one poster which relates to the subject of the chapter. It should be displayed and used for reference throughout the work on the chapter. The poster notes (on the chapter opening page) offer suggestions for how they could be used. There is a black and white version in the book and full-colour version on the digital component for you to print or display on a whiteboard.

Activities

Each section contains two activities. These activities all take the form of a photocopiable page which is in the book and on the digital component for you to display or print out (answers are provided, where appropriate, in the answers document on the digital component). Many of the photocopiable pages have linked interactive activities on the digital component. These interactive activities are designed to act as starter activities to the lesson, giving whole-class support on the information being taught. However, they can also work equally well as plenary activities, reviewing the work the children have just completed.

Workbooks

Accompanying this series is a set of workbooks containing practice activities which are divided into chapters to match the teacher's resource book. Use a combination of the photocopiable pages in this book and the activities in the workbook to help children practise and consolidate comprehension skills. There is also a section of comprehension exercises which use all the comprehension skills learned throughout the book, rather than focusing on a single skill.

Using the CD-ROM

Below are brief guidance notes for using the CD-ROM. For more detailed information, see 'How to use this digital content' on the Main menu.

The CD-ROM follows the structure of the book and contains:

- All of the photocopiable pages.
- All of the poster pages in full colour.
- Answers provided, where relevant.
- Interactive on-screen activities linked to the photocopiable pages.

Getting started

Put the CD-ROM into your CD-ROM drive.

- For Windows users, the install wizard should autorun, if it fails to do so then navigate to your CD-ROM drive. Then follow the installation process.
- For Mac users, copy the disk image file to your hard drive. When it's finished, double click it to mount the disk image. Navigate to the mounted disk image and run the installer. After installation the disk image can be unmounted and the DMG can be deleted from the hard drive.
- To install on a network, please see the ReadMe file located on the CD-ROM (navigate to your drive).

To complete the installation of the program you need to open it and click 'Update' in the pop-up. Please note – this CD-ROM is web-enabled and the content will be downloaded from the internet to your hard-drive to populate the CD-ROM with the relevant resources. This only needs to be done on first use, after this you will be able to use the CD-ROM without an internet connection. If at any point any content is updated you will receive another pop-up upon start up with an internet connection.

Main menu

Here you can access: terms and conditions, registration links, how to use this digital content and credits. To access a specific year group click on the relevant button (NB only titles installed will be available). To browse all installed content click **All resources**.

Chapter menu

This menu provides links to all of the chapters for a specific year group. Clicking on the relevant Chapter icon will take you to the section screen. Clicking on **All resources** will take you to a list of all the resources.

Section screen

Here you can choose the relevant section to take you to its Activity menu. You can also access the posters.

Activity menu

Upon choosing a section, you are taken to a list of resources for that section. Here you can access all of the photocopiable pages related to that section as well as the linked interactive activities.

All resources

All resources lists all of the resources for a year group (if accessed via a Chapter menu) or all of the installed resources (if accessed via the Main menu). You can:

- Select a chapter and/or section by selecting the appropriate title from the drop-down menus.
- Search for key words by typing them into the search box.

To launch a resource, simply click on the **Go** button.

Navigation

The resources all open in separate windows on top of the menu screen. To close a resource, click on the **x** in the top right-hand corner of the screen and this will return you to the menu screen.

Closing a resource will not close the program. However, if you are in a menu screen, then clicking on the **x** will close the program. To return to a previous menu screen, you need to click on the **Back** button.

Teacher settings

In the top left-hand corner of the Main menu screen is a small **T** icon. This is the teacher settings area. It is password protected, the password is: login. This area will allow you to choose the print quality settings for interactive activities and update or refresh content.

Answers

The answers to the photocopiable pages can be found on the CD-ROM in the All resources menu. The pages that have answers are referenced in the 'Digital content' boxes on the teachers' notes pages. Unfortunately, due to the nature of English, not all pages can have answers provided because some activities require the children's own imaginative input or consist of a wider writing task.

Objectives

	Page	Section	English skills objective	To increase their familiarity with a wide range of books...and retell some of these orally.	To identify themes and conventions in a wide range of books.	To ask questions to improve their understanding of a text.	To predict what might happen from details stated and implied.	To identify main ideas drawn from more than one paragraph and summarising these.	To identify how language, structure and presentation contribute to meaning.	To retrieve and record information from non-fiction.
Chapter 1	10	The story beginning	To retell using key questions to highlight the main points at the beginning of a story.	✓	✓	✓				
Chapter 1	14	Problem and resolution	To retell, extending the main theme and 'who', 'what' and 'where' points of a story to include the problem and how the problem is solved (resolution).	✓	✓	✓		✓		✓
Chapter 1	18	Retelling instructions	To organise non-fiction information and to retell it accurately in the correct order.	✓		✓		✓		✓
Chapter 1	22	Sequencing	To organise story information and to retell it in sequence.			✓			✓	
Chapter 2	28	'Who' questions	To identify literal information about characters within pictures and text. To gather, organise and classify this information in order to respond to questions and formulate questions.			✓				
Chapter 2	32	'What' questions	To identify literal information about what the characters and objects are doing. To gather, organise and classify this information in order to respond to and generate questions.			✓				
Chapter 2	36	'Where' questions	To identify literal information about where the characters are within pictures. To gather, organise and classify this information in order to respond to questions and formulate questions.			✓				
Chapter 2	40	'Who', 'what' and 'where' questions	To identify and classify literal key word information about characters, action and place within text. To respond to questions and formulate questions from text.			✓				
Chapter 3	46	Cause and effect	To find clues from images and words that suggest what might happen next.			✓	✓			
Chapter 3	50	Anticipating before and after	To look for clues in text and pictures that suggest what may have happened before and what might happen next.			✓	✓			
Chapter 3	54	Clues from the cover	To look for clues from book covers' pictures and titles to predict what to expect from the story or information inside.		✓	✓	✓			✓
Chapter 3	58	Predicting from images and words	To use picture and word clues to predict outcomes.			✓	✓			

Objectives

Page	Section	English skills objective	To check that the text makes sense to them, discussing their understanding and explaining the meaning of words in context.	To ask questions to improve their understanding of a text.	To draw inferences such as inferring characters' feelings, thoughts and motives from their actions, and justifying inferences with evidence.	To predict what might happen from details stated and implied.	To retrieve and record information from non-fiction.
Chapter 4							
64	Inferred non-fiction clues	To identify and interpret inferred meaning from picture and text clues to better understand the author's meaning and answer inference questions.		✓	✓		✓
68	Seeking evidence clues	To identify inferred meaning from text clues and pictures to use as evidence to support deduction.		✓	✓		
72	Being a text detective	To gather and present evidence that indicates a full understanding of the author's intention.		✓	✓		
76	Asking and answering inference questions	To gather, organise and classify inferred information to formulate questions and answers from text and pictures.		✓	✓		
Chapter 5							
82	What does it mean?	To make sense of unfamiliar words and images using contextual clues and what you know already.	✓	✓			
86	Similar and opposite meanings	To make sense of contextual clues that have similar and opposite meanings.	✓	✓	✓		
90	Skimming and scanning	To answer literal questions from text by skimming and scanning to locate the same words as the key words that appear in the question.	✓	✓			
94	Synonyms and antonyms	To learn how to skim and scan for similar and opposite meanings within text and pictures that link to question key clues. To infer from these clues to answer questions and support deduction.	✓	✓	✓		
Chapter 6							
100	Characters' feelings and actions	To draw on personal experience to interpret characters' emotions and actions within pictures and text to explain what is happening or may happen next.		✓	✓	✓	
104	What you think	To understand that an evaluation question asks you to use your literal and inference skills, and personal experience to think about a character's feelings or actions.		✓	✓		
108	Characters' thoughts	To identify characters' thoughts, feelings and reactions to changing events from word clues to support understanding of evaluation within text.		✓	✓		
112	Evaluation questions	To understand that evaluation questions use a mix of literal, inferred and personal understanding to answer them.		✓	✓		
Chapter 7							
118	Stories	To identify the plot and sequence of events within picture stories and to gather clues and information from non-fiction pictures and text to answer questions.					
123	Fiction and non-fiction	To skim and scan for literal, inferential and evaluative information. To respond to questions by locating compound words, and the same, similar or opposite meanings to key words in the questions.					

Chapter 7 provides revision of all skills covered in the preceding 6 chapters.

Chapter 1
Retelling

Introduction

This chapter teaches children how to retell and summarise effectively. When they use this skill frequently and listen to others retelling daily, their fiction and non-fiction reading comprehension improves significantly. It is a key skill that reflects their real understanding of a text. It also helps children to focus on the specific elements of story structure whether in fiction or non-fiction. In addition, children have to practise summarising and sequencing skills to be able to retell coherently, in a logical sequence and in their own words. For further practice, please see the 'Retelling' section in the Year 4 workbook.

Poster notes

Retelling flowchart (page 9)

A story flowchart is a useful way to support children's retelling. It offers a simple guide summarising beginning, middle and end that helps them to unravel text, focus on the main points and sequence the events within the story narrative. It helps them to:

- concentrate on the theme of the story
- classify the 'who', 'what' and 'where' information in relation to character, action and place details at the beginning
- establish what the problem is for the characters in the middle
- include what happens in the end to give a full summary.

In this chapter

	About each section	About the comprehension activity
The story beginning page 10	Children look at pictures and text to establish who is in the story, what they are doing and where they are.	Children answer literal questions about pictures and text from *Fred* by Posy Simmonds.
Problem and resolution page 14	Children consider problem and resolution within stories.	Children look at a poster about a lost cat and infer meaning from it.
Retelling instructions page 18	Children consider the importance of sequence by looking at instructions.	Children answer questions about 'Boy soup' from *Beware of boys* by Tony Blundell.
Sequencing page 22	Children to think about the structure and sequence of stories.	Children look at the poem 'My cat' by Nigel Gray and answer questions about its structure.

Retelling

Retelling flowchart

Beginning – who, what and where

Theme – main idea

Beginning
Theme – main idea of story/what it revolves around.
Who? – main story characters – **Person.**
What? – what the characters are doing – **Action.**
Where? – where the story happens – **Place.**

Middle – problem

Middle
Problem/conflict – What the main characters want to happen.
Events – How the characters try to solve the problem.

End – solution

End
Resolution/conclusion – Is the problem solved or not solved? How did the story end? How did the main character feel?

Illustrations © 2009, Robin Edmonds/Beehive Illustration.

■SCHOLASTIC
www.scholastic.co.uk

PHOTOCOPIABLE

The story beginning

To retell using key questions to highlight the main points at the beginning of a story.

Background knowledge

A valuable tip for children to remember when retelling a story is to first refer to the overall theme (the subject matter or moral of the story). For example, *This story is about a king and queen who befriend a lonely dragon*. They then need to ask themselves literal questions about the story to present the main points to their audience: *Who is in the story? What are they doing? What is happening? Where are they?* From this basic information the story summary can unfold to include the problem and events leading to the resolution and end. These main points can provide a useful first statement to begin the story retelling, for example: *One day* (Who?) *a king and a queen* (What?) *heard loud screaming and shouting* (Where?) *in the castle grounds*.

Skills

Explain that these activities will help the children to practise gathering the most important points from text and pictures to retell the beginning of a story in three easy steps.

● **Photocopiable page 11 'The lonely dragon'**
  ● Explain to the children that to retell you only need to repeat the main points of a story: the story theme; 'who', 'what' and 'where' information; problem and resolution. Tell the children that they are first going to practise retelling the beginning of a story.
  ● Tell the children the story of 'The lonely dragon' using the photocopiable sheet. Then write the sentence *The dragon sat sobbing below the castle walls* on the board. Discuss what it says and ask them to draw a picture of the scene.

● Ask the children to think carefully about the information within their picture that shows the character ('The dragon'), their actions ('sat sobbing') and place they are in ('below the castle walls'). Explain that if they have included these three elements then they have picked out the main points of the sentence that tells the story.
● Hand out the photocopiable sheet and ask the children to discuss the character, action and place in the picture and underline the 'who', 'what' and 'where' information in the text.
● Ask them to retell the picture information to their partners, reminding them to use the 'who', 'what' and 'where' information.
● Repeat this exercise with the other images in the story flowchart on poster page 9.

Comprehension

● **Photocopiable pages 12 and 13 'Fred'**
  ● Hand out the first photocopiable sheet. Ask the children to read the text and to identify 'who', 'what' and 'where'.
  ● Then hand out the second photocopiable sheet. Explain to the children that they need to answer the questions about the text and pictures in full, and then ask and answer their own 'who', 'what' or 'where' question.

Digital content

On the digital component you will find:
● Printable versions of all three photocopiable pages.
● Answers to 'Fred (2)'.
● Interactive version of 'The lonely dragon'.

The story beginning

The lonely dragon

Once upon a time there lived a young King and a Queen. They ruled their kingdom together and everyone was happy.

One day the King was sitting on his throne when he heard a lot of screaming and shouting outside. The Queen rushed in and told him that a dragon had arrived outside the city walls.

"What do you think we should do?" she asked the King.

"Fetch two of our biggest swords," he said to his manservant.

The manservant returned with an enormous sword for the Queen and an even bigger one for the King. The King and the Queen both ran to the top of the city walls and looked over with their swords at the ready.

Beneath them they saw the huge green dragon. The dragon looked forlorn, tears trickled down its cheeks and every now and then it sobbed.

"Poor thing. I don't want to hurt it," said the King.

"Nor do I," agreed the Queen. "Let's make friends with it."

And they did. The dragon cheered up at once. It had never had any friends before.

The King and the Queen put away their big swords and they all lived happily ever after.

Illustrations © 2009, Robin Edmonds/Beehive Illustration.

SCHOLASTIC
www.scholastic.co.uk   **PHOTOCOPIABLE**   Scholastic English Skills
Comprehension: Year 4   **11**

Name:

Fred (1)

Sophie and Nick sit on the step outside their house feeling sad....

Everyone is sad when they hear the news....

Text and illustrations © 1987, Posy Simmonds.

PHOTOCOPIABLE

■SCHOLASTIC
www.scholastic.co.uk

The story beginning

Fred (2)

1. What is the main theme of this story?

   The main theme of this story is _____

   _____

2. Who do Nick and Sophie talk to about Fred?

   _____

   _____

3. What was wrong with Fred?

   _____

   _____

4. Who is sad when they hear the news?

   _____

   _____

5. Where did Fred like to sleep?

   _____

   _____

6. Your question:

   _____

   _____

   Your answer:

   _____

   _____

Problem and resolution

Objective

To retell, extending the main theme and 'who', 'what' and 'where' points of a story to include the problem and how the problem is solved (resolution).

Background knowledge

Once a child can establish the main theme and locate basic character, action and place information, summarising can be extended to include the problem for the character(s) and how it is solved. This process is helped by showing children how to identify the 'problem' and 'resolution' within picture narrative and text. This section uses non-fiction texts. Most non-fiction real-life stories, reported events and incidents have a problem for the characters to solve and a resolution, just as fictional stories do.

Skills

Explain to the children that the purpose of these activities is to show them how to locate the 'problem' and 'resolution' within pictures and text to retell the whole story.

- **Photocopiable page 15 'What's the problem?'**
  - Explain to the children that retelling non-fiction events and real-life stories requires as much thought as fictional stories about who is involved, what the problem is for them and how they resolve their difficulties with others.
  - To retell a real-life story or event effectively they need to be able to identify what the problem is for the central character(s) and how it is resolved.
  - Hand out the photocopiable sheet. Ask the children to look carefully at the poster of the found tortoise. Ask: *What is the real-life story here?*

- Using poster page 9 'Retelling flowchart', ask the children to write down the theme, and 'who', 'what' and 'where' information on a separate sheet of paper.
- Can they also pinpoint the problems and solutions within the information? Ask: *What was the problem? How was it resolved? Why is it still a problem? What is the final solution?*
- Ask the children to highlight the information on the tortoise poster that points to the problem and possible solution.
- Tell them to complete a flowchart of the tortoise story using this key information.
- Ask the children to write sentences from the information gathered in the flowchart. Then in pairs retell the stories to each other.

Comprehension

- **Photocopiable pages 16 and 17 'Lost pet'**
  - Hand out the first photocopiable sheet. Discuss it together. *What is the problem being experienced?*
  - Provide the children with the second photocopiable sheet. Explain to the children that they need to answer the questions in full sentences. They need to use the information on the poster to answer the questions.
  - Ask them to write their own questions about the problem or resolution.

Digital content

On the digital component you will find:
- Printable versions of all three photocopiable pages.
- Answers to 'Lost pet (2)'.
- Interactive version of 'What's the problem?'

What's the problem?

FOUND TORTOISE
10th October (yesterday).

Found under the big oak trees at the park end of Fairfield Avenue.

Weighs about 10lbs (4.5kg)

Contact:
Charlie Maddison
Fairfield House
Park Road
CM4 8TG
01662 4545457

Can you provide some evidence to prove that it is your tortoise?
(I'm a bit worried because the weather is getting cold and I don't know how to look after tortoises.)

Illustrations © 2009, Robin Edmonds/Beehive Illustration.

Problem and resolution

Lost pet (1)

LOST CAT
Missing since Friday 25th January

MONTY – male, fluffy tabby kitten with a white tip to his tail.
Tiny with fragile health.

He is wearing a red collar with a yellow barrel attached
that contains his name and address.

Belongs to Alfie Graham,
18 Random Road,
Budleigh Salterton
MP4 3TG
01365 268632

£50.00 reward

**PLEASE CHECK ALL OUTBUILDINGS
AND GARAGES**

Photograph © dulezidar/www.istockphoto.com.

PHOTOCOPIABLE   SCHOLASTIC
www.scholastic.co.uk

Problem and resolution

Lost pet (2)

1. Who is concerned about his pet's safety?

_____

2. What has happened to Monty?

_____

_____

3. What will be the main problem if Monty isn't found soon?

_____

_____

4. The owner has done a number of things to help solve the problem. Name three.

_____

_____

_____

_____

5. Your question:

_____

Your answer:

_____

_____

6. Your question:

_____

Your answer:

_____

Retelling instructions

Objective

To organise non-fiction information and to retell it accurately in the correct order.

Background knowledge

To retell instructions in your own words involves a different process to story retelling. This is because the purpose it serves is to direct and provide others with precise information that they will be able to follow easily. This information takes the form of a series of small steps, such as: recipes, directions, games and so on, that need to be retold in the right order for the listener to understand how to complete the task successfully.

It is also important to retell non-fiction information in a logical order so that it makes sense to the listener. To help children to order their thoughts before giving instructions, the following sequencing guide might be useful: *To follow these instructions you must: first... next... then... finally...*

Skills

Explain to the children that the purpose of this activity is to show them how to repeat instructions accurately by putting the information in the right order.

● **Photocopiable page 19 'Fruit trifle'**
  ● Explain to the children that the purpose of retelling instructions is to give directions in your own words, in a logical sequence of small steps that are easy for the listener to understand and to follow.
  ● Tell them that they are going to practise retelling instructions by guiding each other through a recipe for fruit trifle. It is important that their directions are clear otherwise the trifle will be a mess.

● Hand out the photocopiable sheet to pairs of children. Tell them that it is a recipe for fruit trifle that someone has written down in a hurry. It is all jumbled up and needs to be arranged in the correct order.
● Ask them to read the information on the page to a partner. Does it make sense? Can they follow these instructions? Ask them to think about the information that should come first. What do they need to make the recipe?
● Tell them to cut out the strips on the page that contain the ingredients and each instruction.
● Then ask them to rearrange the information strips into logical 'first', 'next' and 'then' order.
● Ask them to retell the instructions to their partners.

Comprehension

● **Photocopiable pages 20 and 21 'Boy soup'**
  ● Hand out the first photocopiable sheet. Ask the children to read it through carefully and consider the order of the instructions.
  ● Give the children the second photocopiable sheet. Ask them to answer the questions in full sentences and to ask and answer their own questions.

Digital content

On the digital component you will find:
● Printable versions of all three photocopiable pages.
● Answers to 'Fruit trifle' and 'Boy soup (2)'.
● Interactive versions of 'Fruit trifle' and 'Boy soup'.

Retelling instructions

Fruit trifle

■ Cut out the instructions below and put them in the correct order. Retell the instructions to a partner.

Arrange fruit on top.
Pieces of sponge soaked in fruit juice.
Remove any pips.
Chop and slice into bite-size bits.
Cartons of custard and cream.
Peel all the fruit.
Any kind of fresh fruit you like.
Put bits of sponge at the bottom of the dish.
Decorate the top with extra bits of fruit.
Pour on custard then the cream.
Keep slices of fruit back to decorate.
Wash the fruit.

Illustrations © 2009, Robin Edmonds/Beehive Illustration.

Name:

Boy soup (1)

Recipe for Boy Soup

Ingredients:

(to serve one greedy wolf)

One boy (medium-sized)
One large iron pot
One tonne of potatoes
One oodle of onions
One wooden tub of turnips
One cartload of carrots
One packet of fruity chews
One wellful of water
One barrel of bricks
One trowel

Method:

1. First catch your boy.
2. Wash him thoroughly, especially behind the ears.
3. Place him firmly in the iron pot.
4. Add water, potatoes, onions, turnips, carrots and fruity chews to taste.
5. Sit on the barrel of bricks and stir with the trowel until Thursday.

Text and illustrations © 1991, Tony Blundell.

PHOTOCOPIABLE **SCHOLASTIC** www.scholastic.co.uk

Retelling instructions

Boy soup (2)

1. What important ingredient do you need before you begin to make this recipe?

_____

_____

2. When do you place your boy in an iron pot?

_____

_____

3. When the boy is in the pot what do you do next?

_____

_____

4. What are you told to do at the end?

_____

_____

5. Your question:

_____

_____

Your answer:

_____

_____

6. Your question:

_____

_____

Your answer:

_____

_____

Sequencing

Objective

To organise story information and to retell it in sequence.

Background knowledge

Like stories, narrative poems have a beginning, middle and an end that is built around a sequence of events. It is useful for children to have a scaffold to retell the sequence of these events in the correct order. The listener will only follow if they hear the main points in the order that they happen, starting from the beginning.

To retell the main points of a story meaningfully, it is helpful for the children to have a sequencing guide that will help them to order their thoughts.
For example:

● **Beginning:** The story is about... (Who? What? Where?)
● **Middle:** The problem is that... What happens is... The characters feel...
● **End:** What happens in the end is...

Skills

These activities give children practice retelling the beginning, middle and end of a story in the correct sequence.

● **Photocopiable page 23 'Seed'**
   ● Hand out the photocopiable sheet and ask the children to look at the pictures and text from left to right. Can they now retell the poem 'Seed' to their partners?
   ● Explain that the poet has used 'personification' to tell the seed's story as if it is a person.

● Discuss the difficulties their partners found understanding the retelling. *Did it have a recognisable beginning, middle or end?* Agree as a class that the pictures and text are in the wrong order. Ask the children to highlight the clues that show them the progression of the poem.
● Tell them to cut out the boxes and arrange them in the correct order using the 'beginning', 'middle' and 'end' labels.
● Next, ask for a volunteer to retell the beginning of the poem in their own words, then someone else to retell the middle and another to retell the end of the poem.
● Now ask the class to retell the whole poem to their partners using the rearranged boxes as a guide. Remind them of the guide above that will help them keep the sequence of the poem in order.

Comprehension

● **Photocopiable pages 24 and 25 'My cat'**
   ● Hand out the first photocopiable sheet. Read the poem together.
   ● Provide the children with the second photocopiable sheet. Ask the children to read the questions, then answer them in full sentences. Remind them to consider beginning, middle and end as they answer the questions and ask and answer their own.

Digital content

On the digital component you will find:
● Printable versions of all three photocopiable pages.
● Answers to 'Seed' and 'My cat (2)'.
● Interactive versions of 'Seed' and 'My cat'.

Sequencing

Seed

■ Cut out the boxes below and arrange them in the correct order to retell the story. Use the labels at the foot of the page to help you.

I hid.
I hid in the dark for weeks, I did
I got fat.
I got fat eating the heat
And drinking the rain.
I got too fat.
I got too fat for my jacket
And my jacket split in two
With a tiny sound like a sneeze,
ah-chooooo.

And I was pleased to see
So many others just like me,
So many of us reaching up,
Making each hand into a cup
To drink the sun and eat the rain.
I know I'll flower, then I'll die.
And I know we'll all begin again.

I put a soft shoot out
And when that soft shoot was strong,
Strong to stand on,
I put out a long thin arm
To see where the air was.

The air was not far above my head.
It took just a week to get there.
When I was there I spread
My thin green fingers to the sun
And the sun was pleased to see me.
And I was pleased to see the sun.

Beginning	Middle 1
Middle 2	End

Text © 2002, Mal Peet; illustrations © 2009, Robin Edmonds/Beehive Illustration.

Name:

My cat (1)

My cat
got fatter
and fatter.
I didn't know
what was the matter.
Then,
know what she did?
She went into the cupboard
and hid.

She was fat when she went in,
but she came out
thin.
I had a peep.
Know what I saw?
Little kittens
all in a heap

-1 - 2 - 3 - 4

My cat's great.

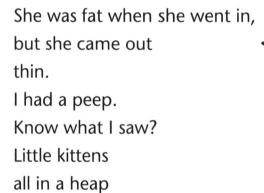

By Nigel Gray

Text © 1987, Nigel Gray; illustrations © Robin Edmonds/Beehive Illustration.

PHOTOCOPIABLE

SCHOLASTIC
www.scholastic.co.uk

Sequencing

My cat (2)

1. Was the cat's owner confused at the beginning of the poem? How do you know that?

_____

_____

2. What does the cat do next that seems strange?

_____

_____

3. What did the cat do before the end of the story to further surprise the owner?

_____

_____

4. How do you think the owner felt when they had a peep in the cupboard?

_____

_____

5. What happens in the end?

_____

_____

6. Your question:

_____

_____

Your answer:

_____

_____

■ SCHOLASTIC   PHOTOCOPIABLE

Chapter 2

Literal questioning

Introduction

The author's literal intention is communicated by key words that 'paint a picture in the reader's head'. These key words are found right there on the page and tell the reader *who* is in the picture or text, *what* they are doing, *where* it is happening (and sometimes *when* it is happening). They provide the reader with the basic story structure (character, action, place) and are the focus for literal questions and answers. Literal questioning is the simplest and most direct of the three question types to answer because literal meaning is obvious to the reader and does not require interpretation. For further practice, please see the 'Literal questioning' section in the Year 4 workbook.

Poster notes

PC Page always right there! (page 27)
This poster offers a guide for the children to follow that helps them to grasp the concept of 'being literal'. It introduces the children to PC Page from the 'Literacy Force' whose job is to patrol the images and sentences in her book and write down everything she sees. She notes down what happens right there in front of her – who is involved, what is happening and where it is happening. The poster serves as a useful classroom prompt throughout Chapter 2.

In this chapter

	About each section	About the comprehension activity
'Who' questions page 28	Children ask and answer questions that focus on who the characters are.	Children answer 'who' questions about *Gulliver* retold by Martin Jenkins.
'What' questions page 32	Children answer questions about what characters and objects are doing.	Children answer and generate their own 'where' questions about *Rapunzel* by Lynn Roberts.
'Where' questions page 36	Children focus on where the characters are in pictures.	Children use a beach map to answer 'where' questions.
'Who', 'what' and 'where' questions page 40	Children consolidate 'who', 'what' and 'where' by looking at them all together.	Children answer a range of literal questions about *The goose who laid the golden eggs*.

Literal questioning

PC Page always right there!

I note down the **who**, **what** and **where** that is right there!

Welcome to Lilliput.

Gulliver stared in disbelief as the six inch high man introduced himself.

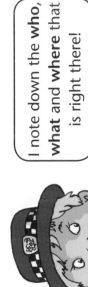

PC Page knows where to look
To write the facts down in her book.
She knows the literal **who**, **what** and **where**.
Are on the page – yes, right there!
She is always on the case
Noting the character, action and place.

PC Page: Who? What? Where? Right there!

Illustrations © 2009, Robin Edmonds/Beehive Illustration.

'Who' questions

Objectives

To identify literal information about characters within pictures and text. To gather, organise and classify this information to respond to questions and formulate questions.

Background knowledge

The simplest of the literal questions to generate and answer are 'who' questions which children develop early on. They are the easiest of the literal questions to recognise and respond to. This may be because they refer to story character(s) that are central to the plot (such as: a person, animal or thing) and can be easily located.

Answers to 'who' questions are quick to check because only the character's identity from the information given on the page is required to replace the 'who' word at the front of the question. The remainder of the sentence remains unchanged to give a full answer. However, children may need practise locating character identity when it is referred to as a pronoun in text.

Skills

Explain to the children that these activities will show them how to find information that will help them to ask and answer 'who' questions.

- **Photocopiable page 29 'Home on the train'**
  - Talk to the children about the purpose of questions. *What does a question look like?*
  - Ask them in pairs to explain why they would ask a literal 'who' question about a story. What would they focus on to ask the question? For example: people, animals or things in a story.
  - Discuss the difference between an answer (which is a statement and something you know) such as: *The family is sad*; and a question (that asks about something you want to know) such as: *Who is sad?*

- Remind the children that you simply replace the subject at the beginning of the statement with 'who' and add a question mark at the end to create a question.
- Model this further by writing a statement on the board for the children to change into a 'who' question and then an answer. You can do this as a game. Put the children into teams and ask the teams to change the statements into 'who' questions. The children can compete for points.
- Hand out the photocopiable sheet. Ask the children to look at the picture, read the caption and circle the 'who' information in the text and picture. Remind them to include any pronouns.
- Tell the children to follow the examples given and practise asking and answering 'who' questions from the information they have circled on the page. Remind them that it is helpful to write their responses in full sentences to guide their answers.

Comprehension

- **Photocopiable pages 30 and 31 'Gulliver'**
  - Hand out the first photocopiable sheet. Ask the children to look at the picture and read the text carefully. Tell them to circle the 'who' information they find.
  - Hand out the second photocopiable sheet and ask them to use the information they have highlighted to answer the questions and then to generate their own questions.

Digital content

On the digital component you will find:
- Printable versions of all three photocopiable pages.
- Answers to 'Home on the train' and 'Gulliver (2)'.
- Interactive version of 'Home on the train'.

'Who' questions

Home on the train

■ Read the text and look at the picture. Find the **who** information. Then answer the question and write the answer below.

■ Can you think of any other **who** questions? Write them on another sheet of paper and ask your partner to answer them.

The family are **sad** to see them go. They are going back home on the train after a long stay of four weeks. Ben, Kim and little Tina wave goodbye. They know they won't see them again for a whole year. Granny and Granddad live in Australia and they live in England. Even the dog is upset. He doesn't like to see the family unhappy.

"They will be back again before we know it," said Mum.

Question: Who is sad?

Answer: The family are sad.

Question: Who is going back home?

Answer:

_____

Question:

_____

Answer: The dog doesn't like to see the family unhappy.

Illustrations © 2009, Robin Edmonds/Beehive Illustration.

Name:

'Who' questions

Gulliver (1)

By being as gentle and friendly as possible, I hoped to be allowed my freedom. The people quickly lost all fear of me, often coming to dance on my hand. The children would even play hide-and-seek in my hair.

Text © 2004, Martin Jenkins; illustration © 2004, Chris Riddell.

PHOTOCOPIABLE   SCHOLASTIC   www.scholastic.co.uk

'Who' questions

Gulliver (2)

1. Who quickly lost all fear of Gulliver?

   _____

2. Who was playing hide-and-seek in the picture?

   _____

3. Whose hair were the children playing in?

   _____

4. Your question:

   _____

   Your answer:

   _____

5. Your question:

   _____

   Your answer:

   _____

6. Your question:

   _____

   Your answer:

   _____

7. Your question:

   _____

   Your answer:

   _____

'What' questions

Objectives

To identify literal information about what the characters and objects are doing. To gather, organise and classify this information to respond to and generate questions.

Background knowledge

Questions that ask 'what' are rather more awkward to ask and answer than 'who' questions. This is because in addition to the characters' actions, 'what' also asks about objects and events within a story. It is important that the children understand the difference between generating questions about characters' actions and objects within a story and asking questions about what is happening in a story. The first is only asking about a detail in the story and requires a verb or noun answer, while the second is asking for information about a greater chunk of the story and requires a combination of 'who', 'what' and 'where' to give a full response (see poster page 9 'Retelling flowchart').

'What' questions also offer only part of a guide for a response. The words need to be rearranged to make a statement. For example: *What is Sam **doing** in the pool? Sam is **swimming** in the pool.*

Skills

Explain to the children that these activities will show them how to find information that will help them to ask and answer 'what' questions.

- **Photocopiable page 33 'Holiday'**
  - Ask the children to explain the difference between 'who' and 'what' questions. Then show them a statement such as: Sarah *listened* carefully. Ask them to turn this into a 'what' question: *What did Sarah do?* Remind them that when you need to know what someone is doing, or what an object is, you need to ask 'what' at the beginning of the question.

- Choose a picture from an action story and hold it up for the class to see. Invite them to ask questions about the characters in the picture. For example: *What are the characters doing? What are they wearing? What are they using in the picture?* Ask them for a full answer and not just one word.
- Hand out the photocopiable sheet. Remind the children to ask themselves the following questions: *What are the characters doing or going to do? What are they using or wearing?* Ask them to circle the 'what' information on the page. Tell them to then follow the question examples given to generate their own questions and answers using the circled information.
- Explain that the subject of a 'what' question should always begin the answer because you are asking about the character or its actions.

Comprehension

- **Photocopiable pages 34 and 35 'Rapunzel'**
  - Hand out the first photocopiable sheet and ask the children to talk about the actions and objects which they can see.
  - Then ask the children to complete the second photocopiable sheet in full sentences.

Digital content

On the digital component you will find:
- Printable versions of all three photocopiable pages.
- Answers to 'Holiday' and 'Rapunzel (2)'.
- Interactive versions of 'Holiday' and 'Rapunzel'.

'What' questions

Holiday

■ Complete the answer and question examples below. Then write your own **what** questions and answers about the picture and text.

Every summer my friend Amir and his family go on holiday with us. Here we are setting up camp for two weeks. Amir is helping his mum to set up for supper and the rest of his family are collecting wood for the fire. Mum and Dad are showing my brother Gareth how to put our large tent up. I am the one knocking the tent pegs in. My nan is in charge of our dog to stop him getting in the way.

■ Remember to begin the question with **what** and answer with the subject of the question.

Question: What *does Amir's family* **do** *every summer?*

Answer: Amir's family **go on holiday** every summer.

Question: What is the lady with the dog wearing to shade her eyes?

Answer:

_____

Question:

_____

Answer: Amir's family are collecting wood for the fire.

Illustrations © 2009, Robin Edmonds/Beehive Illustration.

'What' questions

Rapunzel (1)

To keep Rapunzel quiet (and to make herself seem nice, which she was not) Edna brought Rapunzel second-hand magazines and records and occasionally allowed her to watch television. "When you are older," Edna lied, "I'll take you out and show you the city, but it's not safe for you on your own."

Rapunzel believed every word, for she knew nothing of the world.

Text and illustrations © 2003, Lynn Roberts and David Roberts.

PHOTOCOPIABLE   SCHOLASTIC
www.scholastic.co.uk

'What' questions

Rapunzel (2)

1. What is Edna doing while Rapunzel is reading her magazine?

    _____

    _____

2. What did Edna do to make herself seem nice?

    _____

    _____

3. What is Edna saying to Rapunzel that is a lie?

    _____

    _____

4. Your 'what' question:

    _____

    _____

    Your answer:

    _____

    _____

5. Your 'what' question:

    _____

    _____

    Your answer:

    _____

    _____

'Where' questions

Objectives

To identify literal information about where the characters are within pictures. To gather, organise and classify this information to respond to questions and formulate questions.

Background knowledge

Children find that literal 'where' questions are quite straightforward to generate and respond to. These questions ask the reader to either locate the whereabouts of characters and objects or to identify places and settings that are there on the page. It is helpful for the children to know that the subject of a 'where' enquiry is usually at the end of a question. For example, in a question such as: *Where is Jane?* 'Jane' is the subject and to respond they simply need to begin their answer with the person's name, pronoun or noun and add the 'where' information at the end, for example: *Jane is at school.* Useful vocabulary for 'where' questions that explain the location of characters and objects in relation to other things are: 'next to', 'beside', 'behind', 'opposite', 'outside', 'inside' and 'near'.

Skills

Explain to the children that these activities will show them how to find information that will help them to ask and answer 'where' literal questions.

- **Photocopiable page 37 'Party invitation'**
  - Explain to the children that when you need to know where someone is in text or pictures, you need to ask 'where' at the beginning of the question. The information that gives the answer to the question is right there in the story.

- Tell them that sometimes when they are asked about the whereabouts of a character or object, they need to explain their whereabouts in relation to other things, for example: *Where is the Garden Centre? The Garden Centre is **opposite** the road to Fallowfields Village.*
- Hand out the photocopiable sheet. Ask the children to look at the party directions and think about where the places are in relation to each other before they answer the questions.
- Finally ask them to generate their own questions and answers from the directions on the map.

Comprehension

- **Photocopiable pages 38 and 39 'Seaside map'**
  - Hand out the first photocopiable sheet. Ask the children to study the map and orally frame some questions using prepositions to a partner.
  - Hand out the second photocopiable sheet. Ask the children to write the answers to the questions in full sentences and to generate their own 'where' questions.

Digital content

On the digital component you will find:
- Printable versions of all three photocopiable pages.
- Answers to 'Party invitation' and 'Seaside map (2)'.
- Interactive versions of 'Party invitation' and 'Seaside map'.

'Where' questions

Party invitation

■ Use the party invitation map to complete the answer and question in full and write your own **where** questions and answers on a separate sheet of paper.

Parents - please park your cars in the driveway and in the field behind the house

■ The words in the box are useful words to explain the whereabouts of characters and objects in relation to other things.

next to	near	behind	outside
opposite	beside	inside	

Question: Where is the Garden Centre?

Answer: The Garden Centre is **opposite the road to Fallowfields Village**.

Question: Where is Jo's house?

Answer:

_____

Question:

_____

Answer: Parents have been asked to park in the driveway or in the field behind the house.

Illustrations © 2009, Robin Edmonds/Beehive Illustration.

Name:

'Where' questions

Seaside map (1)

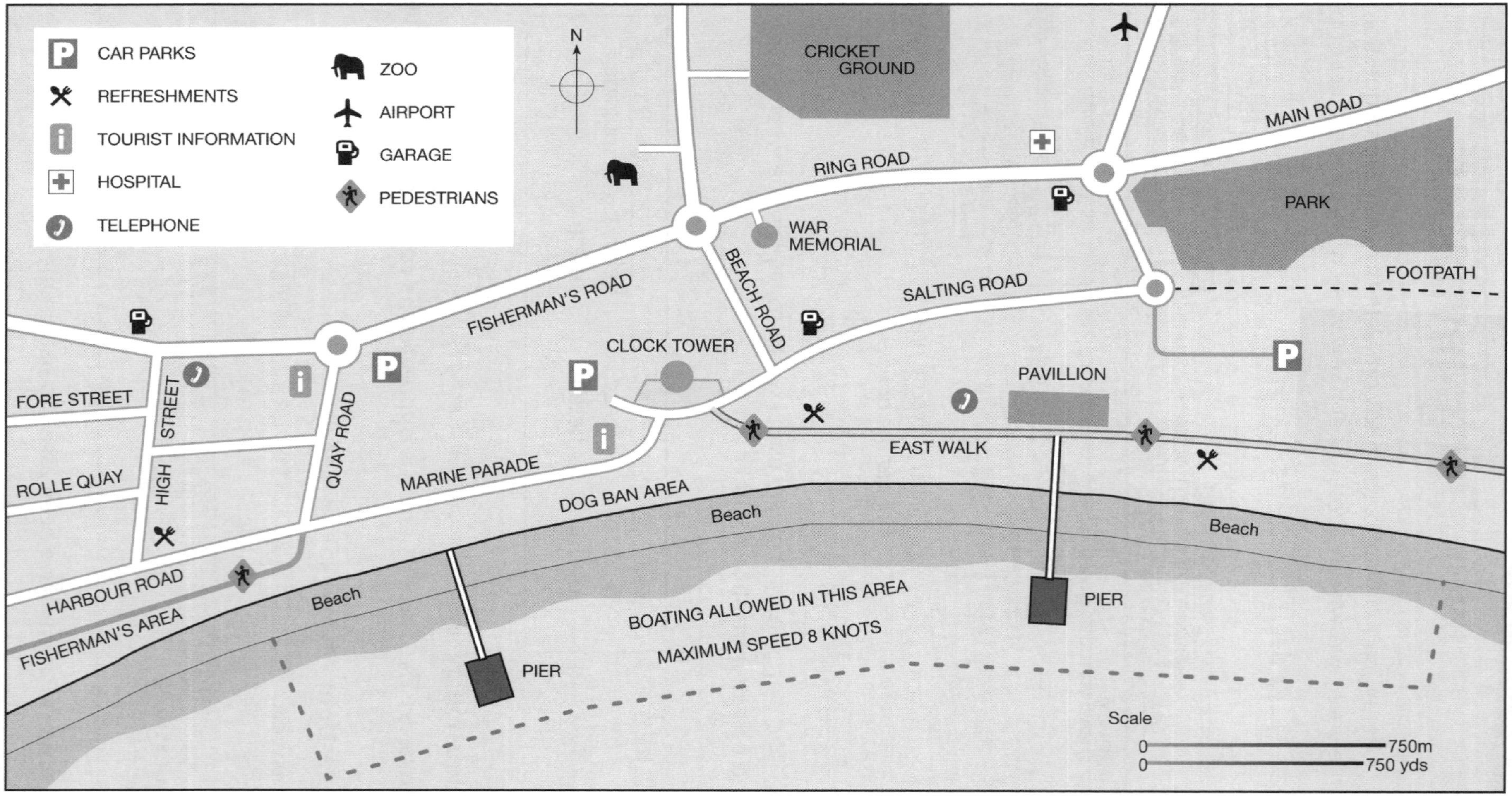

Legend:
- CAR PARKS
- REFRESHMENTS
- TOURIST INFORMATION
- HOSPITAL
- TELEPHONE
- ZOO
- AIRPORT
- GARAGE
- PEDESTRIANS

Scale: 750m / 750 yds

Illustrations © 2009, Redmoor Design.

PHOTOCOPIABLE — SCHOLASTIC — www.scholastic.co.uk

'Where' questions

Seaside map (2)

1. Where can you get refreshments?

   _____

2. Where are vessels allowed to go within a speed of 8 knots?

   _____

3. Your 'where' question:

   _____

   Your answer:

   _____

4. Your 'where' question:

   _____

   Your answer:

   _____

5. Your 'where' question:

   _____

   Your answer:

   _____

6. Your 'where' question:

   _____

   Your answer:

   _____

■SCHOLASTIC
www.scholastic.co.uk   **PHOTOCOPIABLE**   *Scholastic English Skills*
Comprehension: Year 4   **39**

'Who', 'what' and 'where' questions

Objectives

To identify and classify literal key word information about characters, action and place within text.
To respond to questions and formulate questions from text.

Background knowledge

This section asks children to use the literal skills they have learned in the previous sections of this chapter to ask and answer a combination of 'who', 'what' and 'where' questions from text and an accompanying picture. To do this they need first to practise identifying and classifying the literal key words that are associated with character, action and place on the page.

Remind the children that questions usually begin with 'who', 'what' or 'where' and that the literal information and answers are right there in the text. Some questions ask the reader to gather literal information from different parts of the text to give full answers.

Skills

Explain to the children that these activities will show them how to gather 'who', 'what' and 'where' information correctly to ask and answer literal questions from text and pictures.

- **Photocopiable page 41 'The dog and the bone'**
  - Remind the children of the skills they have been learning and practise some 'who', 'what' and 'where' questions. Explain that texts and pictures contain all three of these elements.

- Provide an example sentence such as: *The dog ran off from the butcher's shop.* Ask the children to identify the literal 'who', 'what' and 'where' questions they want to ask about a piece of text. It is useful to highlight the key words that are associated with each one in different coloured pen; for example: 'dog' (who), 'ran off' (what) 'from the butcher's shop' (where).
- Hand out the photocopiable sheet and ask the children to read the text that accompanies the picture. Then ask them to identify and highlight the 'who', 'what' and 'where' key words in different coloured pens.
- Next ask them to classify this information by putting the 'who', 'what' and 'where' information in the appropriate columns that are provided.
- Finally, ask them to generate their own questions and answers from the information they have gathered from the text on a separate sheet of paper.

Comprehension

- **Photocopiable pages 42 and 43 'The goose who laid the golden eggs'**
  - Hand out the first photocopiable sheet. Suggest the children highlight the characters, action and places in different colours within the text as this will help them to answer the questions.
  - Hand out the second photocopiable sheet and ask the children to answer the questions in full. Ask them to write their own 'who', 'what' and 'where' questions.

Digital content

On the digital component you will find:
- Printable versions of all three photocopiable pages.
- Answers to 'The dog and the bone' and 'The goose who laid the golden eggs (2)'.
- Interactive version of 'The dog and the bone'.

The dog and the bone

A dog ran off with a juicy bone from the butcher's shop one day. As he made his escape over the river he saw himself reflected in the water below. Thinking that it was a different dog with another bone, he snapped to grab at the treasure. In moments the bone he was carrying was in the deep water and the 'other' prize was gone. His greed had left him with nothing.

■ Read the story and highlight **who**, **what** and **where**. Put these words in the right columns below.

Who	What (doing)	Where
Example: *dog*	*ran off with a bone*	*from the butcher's shop*

■ Use the information in the table to create questions. For example:

Question: Who ran off with a bone?
Answer: The dog ran off with a bone.

Question:

_____

Answer:

_____

Illustrations © 2009, Robin Edmonds/Beehive Illustration.

Name:

The goose who laid the golden eggs (1)

The next morning, the goose laid another golden egg. And she kept laying one egg after another until the farmer had filled a basket with them. Soon the farmer and his wife had become quite well off. They wore fine clothes and rode to market on horses. They ate fresh food out of expensive bowls. In the summer, they repaired and re-painted the cottage and built a dairy next to it, where they kept a herd of cows.

Text © 2005, Saviour Pirotta; illustrations © 2005, Richard Johnson.

PHOTOCOPIABLE **SCHOLASTIC** www.scholastic.co.uk

'Who', 'what' and 'where' questions

The goose who laid the golden eggs (2)

1. Who is in the picture?

_____

_____

2. What had the goose laid the next morning?

_____

3. Where did the farmer and his wife keep their cows?

_____

_____

4. Your 'who' question:

_____

Your answer:

_____

5. Your 'what' question:

_____

Your answer:

_____

6. Your 'where' question:

_____

Your answer:

_____

Chapter 3

Prediction

Introduction

The purpose of this chapter is to show children how they anticipate from context clues; and make logical links and connections with the author's intention and their own personal world to justify their deductions. Prediction encourages children to think for themselves and modify their thinking as the evidence in a story unfolds. However, to gain the most from their prediction skills they need to have an understanding of how and why it impacts on their comprehension and enjoyment of reading. It is important for them to practise predicting before, during and after reading, checking and modifying their predictions as they read. For further practice, please see the 'Prediction' section in the Year 4 workbook.

Poster notes

Forensic Fred the police predictor (page 45)
Prediction prepares the children for the important rank of text detective. It makes them deduce possible outcomes from clues on the page that are like fingerprints left at the scene of a crime – they point to who is involved, what they have been doing, where they have been, what may happen next and why.

Forensic Fred is a useful analogy to help children grasp the tricky concept of foretelling from evidence and justifying reasons given from the clues they have gathered that link to prior knowledge. The poster presents the middle of a story that suggests what may happen next from a variety of clues left in the text and picture.

In this chapter

	About each section	About the comprehension activity
Cause and effect page 46	Children gather cause and effect clues that suggest the reasons for why things happen.	Children answer literal questions about an African story and then they predict the outcome.
Anticipating before and after page 50	Children are encouraged to make logical predictions help monitor their comprehension.	Children make predictions from clues to answer and ask questions about *Beware of girls* by Tony Blundell.
Clues from the cover page 54	Children make predictions from book covers about the contents of the books.	Children use the cover of *The three little wolves* by Eugene Trivizas to answer and formulate questions.
Predicting from images and words page 58	Children are taught to make meaningful links between words and images to predict story outcomes.	Children predict the outcome from clues in 'A lesson' by Brian Morse to answer and generate questions.

Prediction

Forensic Fred the police predictor

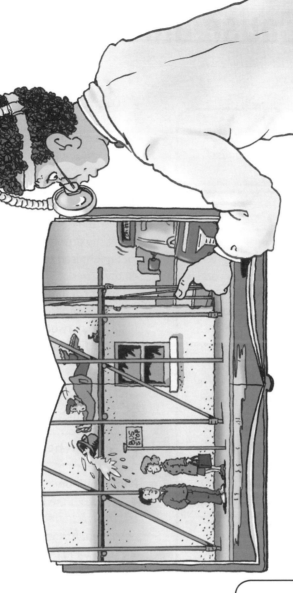

Lovely sunshine! At least we won't get wet today.

Forensic Fred can see where a story might have begun or where it might end.

I ask **why** questions to predict what will happen next from what I know. I can say **how** I know from the clues I find.

From what I know linked to picture clues and text. I guess what went before or what might happen next...

Illustrations © 2009, Robin Edmonds/Beehive Illustration.

■SCHOLASTIC
www.scholastic.co.uk   **PHOTOCOPIABLE**

Cause and effect

Objective

To find clues from images and words that suggest what might happen next.

Background knowledge

To be able to understand and predict story outcomes children need to explain how actions produce consequences and how a series of incidents can be created from one action. This invaluable investigative skill helps them to calculate what may have happened before or what may happen next. It relies on a process of thinking, questioning and reasoning that makes links with their prior knowledge, personal experience and the clues that are offered by the author and illustrator.

It also enables them to make the necessary links that explain how cause and effect works. For example: *If a character takes this action, this might happen because…* or *if this has happened, this might happen next.* To achieve the most from this process they need to make predictions before, during and after reading, checking and modifying them as they read to gain a full understanding of the author's meaning and intention.

Skills

Explain that these activities will show the children how to predict the flow of events in a story narrative.

● **Photocopiable page 47 'One thing leads to another'**

  ● Talk to the children about the purpose of prediction and how some actions have outcomes that can be anticipated. For example if you fall asleep on a bus you will probably miss your stop.

● Discuss everyday cause and effect situations. Encourage the children to talk about things that have happened to them because of their actions or the actions of others. For example if your mum loses the house keys you will both be locked out.

● Hand out the photocopiable sheet. Talk about how flowchart 1 demonstrates how one thing can lead to another. Ask the children to talk in pairs about the possible consequences from actions taken that might lead to the final outcome. Then fill in the empty boxes.

● Tell them that the title of flowchart 2 indicates the theme of the story and the first two boxes give them the story beginning. Ask them to complete the remainder of flowchart 2 boxes based on each other's experience and knowledge. Can they anticipate the chain of actions and outcomes that might have been caused by mum losing her keys?

● Ask them to explain the final outcome.

Comprehension

● **Photocopiable pages 48 and 49 'African story'**

  ● Hand out the first photocopiable sheet and ask the children to discuss the text and predict any possible outcomes.

  ● Then hand out the second photocopiable sheet and ask the children to read the questions carefully before answering them. They also need to generate and answer their own questions.

Digital content

On the digital component you will find:

● Printable versions of all three photocopiable pages.

● Answers to 'One thing leads to another' and 'African story (2)'.

● Interactive version of 'One thing leads to another'.

Cause and effect

One thing leads to another

■ Look at flowchart 1. Describe to a partner how one thing leads to another. Complete flowchart 2. Use the clues in the box to help you.

| break   plant on window sill   sister's toys on floor   trip over   slippery floor |
| dog greeting with wagging tail   small open window   knock over |

Flowchart 1: A long way home

| Run for a bus. |

↓

| Just make it. |

↓

| Tired and drowsy. Nod off. |

↓

| Miss stop. |

↓

| Mother and screaming baby get on the bus. |

↓

| Wake up. |

↓

| Get off at next stop. |

↓

| Get on another bus back to right stop. |

↓

| Finally back home. |

Flowchart 2: Breaking in with Mum

| Mum has lost her keys. |

↓

| Oh no! We're locked out! |

↓

| |

↓

| |

↓

| |

↓

| |

↓

| |

↓

| |

↓

| Mum opening door to pick me up from the floor! |

■SCHOLASTIC   PHOTOCOPIABLE

Name:

Cause and effect

African story (1)

The first tree he came to was growing right in front of a great slab of rock. He decided to rest in its shade for a while before setting off on the last leg of his journey. As he sat down he felt something dripping on to his arm from above. He looked up and saw that it was water. Quickly he rummaged in his bag and pulled out his drinking bowl. What luck to find a spring, he thought. He held up his bowl and it filled quickly, but just as he was about to take a drink, a dove flew at him and with a flurry of its wings knocked the bowl out of his hands. All the water spilled out.

Illustration © 1994, Gregory Alexander.

PHOTOCOPIABLE **SCHOLASTIC**
www.scholastic.co.uk

Cause and effect

African story (2)

1. Do you think the man is on a dangerous journey? Why do you say that?

   _____

   _____

2. Explain why you think the dove knocked the bowl out of the man's hands.

   _____

   _____

3. Predict what you think will happen next to the man and why.

   _____

   _____

4. Your prediction question:

   _____

   Your answer:

   _____

   _____

5. Your prediction question:

   _____

   Your answer:

   _____

   _____

6. Your prediction question:

   _____

   Your answer:

   _____

   _____

Anticipating before and after

To look for clues in text and pictures that suggest what may have happened before and what might happen next.

Background knowledge

Prediction provides children with the perfect opportunity to monitor their comprehension. Context clues help them to make personal links with the author's intention based on what they already know, to predict what has gone before and to think ahead logically as they read to calculate what will happen next. It engages them in ideas and stories, absorbs them in what is possible and asks them to make reasoned justifications for their thinking.

'Think aloud' talk helps children to consider the likely progression of events and can really help them to meaningfully and logically anticipate consequences for characters and events in fiction and non-fiction.

Skills

Explain to the children that these activities will show them how to predict what has happened before and what might happen next from the picture and word clues.

● **Photocopiable page 51 'What has happened?'**
  ● Explain to the children that when they predict it asks them to not only think ahead, but also to guess what may have happened before.
  ● Tell them that they can make predictions from very little information as long as they are able to link the information to their own experience and knowledge.

● Hand out the photocopiable sheet and ask the children to talk about the picture and word clues that link to the boy's position in the picture. Ask questions such as: *Why is he on all fours? What was he doing before this? Was he exhausted and catching his breath back? Why would he be doing this? Where might this be happening?*
● Tell them to make their predictions and write them down on a separate sheet of paper. Ask them to give detailed reasons for what may have happened to him and what they think might happen next.

Comprehension

● **Photocopiable pages 52 and 53 'Beware of girls'**
  ● Give the children the first photocopiable sheet. Ask them to circle the clues in the picture and text that suggest what may happen next.
  ● Hand out the second photocopiable sheet and ask them to answer the questions and generate their own questions and answers.

Digital content

On the digital component you will find:
● Printable versions of all three photocopiable pages.
● Answers to 'Beware of girls (2).
● Interactive version of 'What has happened?'.

Anticipating before and after

What has happened?

■ Can you predict from the word clues why the boy is in this position in the picture? What do you think happened to him before this? What do you think might happen next? Write your ideas on another sheet of paper.

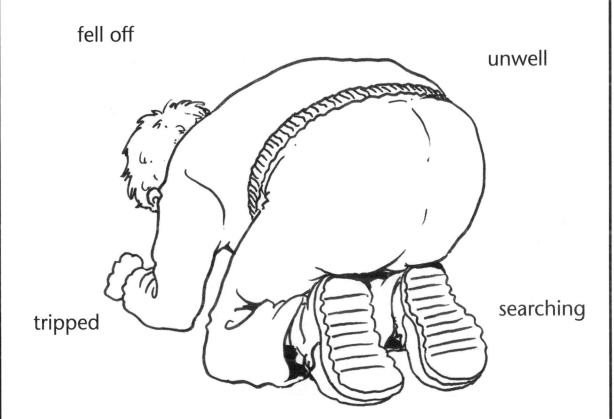

exercising

fell off

unwell

tripped

searching

in a race

Illustrations © 2009, Robin Edmonds/Beehive Illustration.

Beware of girls (1)

Once upon a dark, damp evening deep in the forest, a hungry wolf sat in his cave reading a book about little girls and grandmas.

The wolf was not very good at reading, but the pictures made him feel very hungry indeed!

And they gave the wolf a brilliant idea!

Text and illustration © 2002, Tony Blundell.

Anticipating before and after

Beware of girls (2)

1. Why do you think the wolf should 'beware of girls' as the title suggests?

   _____

   _____

2. Why do you think the pictures in the book made the wolf feel even hungrier?

   _____

   _____

3. What do you think the wolf's brilliant idea was?

   _____

   _____

4. Your prediction question:

   _____

   _____

   Your answer:

   _____

   _____

5. Your prediction question:

   _____

   _____

   Your answer:

   _____

   _____

Clues from the cover

Objective

To look for clues from book covers' pictures and titles to predict what to expect from the story or information inside.

Background knowledge

This section builds on the skills learned in the two previous ones. It shows how discussion about picture and word clues from a book cover is a particularly effective way to elicit predictions from children. Children enjoy making predictions about the contents of a book because it offers them an opportunity to use their investigative and interpretative skills and personal knowledge. From the cover they are able to figure out whether the contents are fiction or non-fiction, and from the title and pictures whether it is a theme or subject they like or already know about. It also tells them what sort of vocabulary they may need to know. The book title often provides key word clues about the contents and theme of the book, whereas the cover picture tends to offer more inferred information about the characters and events inside.

Skills

Explain to the children that these activities will show them how to anticipate story narrative or non-fiction subject matter from clues given in titles and pictures.

- **Photocopiable page 55 'Book covers'**
  - Give the children a range of fiction and non-fiction cover examples to look at and to discuss. Tell them that the purpose of the title and picture on a cover is to offer clues about the book's contents.

- Explain that non-fiction books generally have literal titles and photographs that inform about the subject matter on the cover.
- However, story books tend to rely on an inferred title and illustrations to indicate the story theme and contents.
- Hand out the photocopiable sheet and ask the children to look at the mix of fiction and non-fiction book titles on the page. Ask them to sort the titles into the boxes labelled 'fiction' and 'non-fiction' and explain why.
- Ask the children in pairs to choose a title (or make up their own) and highlight the key words in the chosen title. What do they think the book might be about from this information?
- Using the title information, ask them to illustrate a cover that suggests the contents of the book on a separate sheet of paper.
- Then ask them to write what they think the book is about – using 'who', 'what' and 'where' and the clues given in the cover title and picture to guide their explanation.

Comprehension

- **Photocopiable pages 56 and 57 'Three little wolves'**
  - Hand out the first photocopiable sheet and ask the children to look at and talk about the cover.
  - Once they have done this, give them the second photocopiable sheet and ask them to answer the questions and generate their own.

Digital content

On the digital component you will find:
- Printable versions of all three photocopiable pages.
- Answers to 'Book covers' and 'Three little wolves (2)'.
- Interactive version of 'Book covers'.

Clues from the cover

Book covers

■ Read the book titles. Sort them into the boxes headed non-fiction and fiction. Complete the sentences about why you think they are non-fiction or fiction.

■ Choose a title and design a cover for it. Describe the contents of the book.

Book titles
Wolves   Wolf Soup   The Worried Wolf   Day in the Life of a Wolf Wolves – Endangered Species   Wilf the Wolf

Non-fiction	Fiction
_____	_____
_____	_____
_____	_____
_____	_____

I think they are non-fiction books because

_____

_____

_____

I think they are fiction books because

_____

_____

_____

SCHOLASTIC
www.scholastic.co.uk   **PHOTOCOPIABLE**   **Scholastic English Skills**
Comprehension: Year 4   **55**

Three little wolves (1)

 EUGENE TRIVIZAS 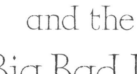 HELEN OXENBURY

The
Three Little Wolves
and the
Big Bad Pig

Illustration © 1993, Helen Oxenbury.

PHOTOCOPIABLE　　**SCHOLASTIC**
www.scholastic.co.uk

Clues from the cover

Three little wolves (2)

1. What sort of book do you think this is? Why do you say that?

_____

_____

2. Who do you think the other character in the book might be? Describe what you think he would look like and why.

_____

_____

3. What do you think the story is about? Why do you say that?

_____

_____

4. From the clues on the cover, what do you think might happen to the main characters in the end? Why do you say that?

_____

_____

5. Your prediction question:

_____

Your answer:

_____

6. Your prediction question:

_____

Your answer:

_____

S C H O L A S T I C
www.scholastic.co.uk   **PHOTOCOPIABLE**

Predicting from images and words

Objective

To use picture and word clues to predict outcomes.

Background knowledge

Although words provide their own images on the page for the reader to visualise and predict, when children are still learning to read, they find it helpful to clarify meanings and ideas via a combination of inferred text clues and descriptive picture information. This information then encourages them to take greater meaning from written stories and non-fiction and helps them to more easily identify with story characters and their problems. It also prompts them to make predictions about the story from their own experience and knowledge.

This section draws on the prediction skills that the children have already learned in this chapter. It encourages them to make meaningful links from a combination of picture and word clues to anticipate outcomes that reflect on the author's intention.

Skills

Explain to the children that these activities will show them how to predict possible outcomes from combined key word clues and images.

- **Photocopiable page 59 'What's inside?'**
  - Explain to the children that words and pictures together offer clues and meaning that can help the reader to make predictions and better understand the author's ideas and intentions.
  - Hand out the photocopiable sheet and ask them in pairs to look at and discuss the images in the picture boxes.

- Explain that it is Christmas Eve and all the gift tags have come off the wrapped presents under the tree and need to be sorted and re-labelled correctly. Can they predict what each present is from its shape?
- Ask them to read the tags and underline the clues in the messages that will help them to identify the gift and who it is for. Then following the example on the page, ask them to link the names to the wrapped shapes and write down what the presents are and why they think they are being given to each person.

Comprehension

- **Photocopiable pages 60 and 61 'A lesson'**
  - Hand out both photocopiable sheets. Ask the children to find clues in the text that link to the pictures and highlight these.
  - Then ask them to answer the questions and generate their own questions and answers.

Digital content

On the digital component you will find:
- Printable versions of all three photocopiable pages.
- Answers to 'What's inside?' and 'A lesson (2)'.
- Interactive versions of 'What's inside?' and 'A lesson'.

What's inside?

■ The tags of these presents have fallen off. Can you match the presents with the correct tags? Write the correct tag below the present.

To Tom so he can get some exercise.

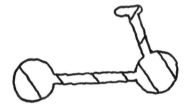

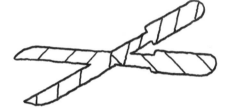

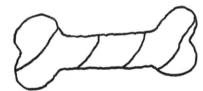

To Hunter who is always hungry.

To Katie who loves scooting about.

To Dad who wants to join the cricket club.

To Grandma who loves wide brims.

To Mum who enjoys her garden.

Illustrations © 2009, Robin Edmonds/Beehive Illustration.

Name:

A lesson (1)

Darren took all
the labels off
the tins in Mummy's
shopping bag.

He sorted them
like teacher had,
red and yellow,
green and blue.

Tonight the dog
had soup for tea,
the cat had beans
and Darren had

Whiskas.
He said it
tasted horrible
on toast.

By Brian Morse

Text © 1998, Brian Morse; Illustrations © 2009, Robin Edmonds/Beehive Illustration.

PHOTOCOPIABLE

Predicting from images and words

A lesson (2)

1. Why do you think Darren's teacher showed them how to sort labels from tins into piles?

_____

_____

2. Which of the food tins do you think were difficult to recognise when Darren took off the labels? Why do you say that?

_____

_____

3. Explain where you think Darren went wrong when he sorted the food tin labels into four different piles.

_____

_____

4. What do you predict happened when Mummy found the tins without their labels? Why do you say that?

_____

_____

5. What do you predict happens in this story? Why do you say that?

_____

_____

_____

6. Your prediction question:

_____

_____

Your answer:

_____

_____

SCHOLASTIC
www.scholastic.co.uk   **PHOTOCOPIABLE**   **Scholastic English Skills**
Comprehension: Year 4   **61**

Chapter 4

Inference

Introduction

This chapter focuses on how to use prediction and justification skills to gain a deeper understanding of the author's meaning and intention. It shows children how to identify the inference clues that highlight the author's hidden and implied meaning and how to justify their deductions by using evidence to back up what they have inferred. This procedure also helps them to identify the difference between being literal and using inference to gather information to ask and answer questions. For further practice, please see the 'Inference' section in the Year 4 workbook.

Poster notes

Being a text detective (page 63)
The Text Detective can go further in his text and picture investigation than PC Page the literal officer. The Text Detective thinks and searches for key clues that are hidden and finds the evidence from the pictures and text to prove his case.

The poster is a useful classroom display to use throughout this chapter as the Text Detective analogy helps to remind the children of the thinking involved in inferential enquiry.

In this chapter

	About each section	About the comprehension activity
Inferred non-fiction clues page 64	Children identify images and words that are inferred.	Children identify whether they are answering literal or inferred questions about a helicopter rescue.
Seeking evidence clues page 68	Children gather inferred information and evidence from picture narrative and text.	Children answer questions about *The children who smelled a rat* by Allan Ahlberg to explain how they know what is happening.
Being a text detective page 72	Children present evidence to justify answers given to inference questions.	Children provide reasoned answers to questions about *I love guinea pigs* by Dick King-Smith.
Asking and answering inference questions page 76	Children ask and answer inference questions using key words.	*The sea monster* by Chris Wormell presents clues from which the children can generate their own questions with justified answers.

Inference

Being a text detective

 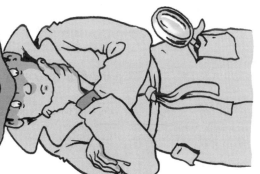

The Text Detective

I arrive on the story scene
After PC Page has been
I search in text and pictures too
To ask **how** and **why** about each clue
I skim and scan as I go.
Gathering evidence to show
how I know.

Illustrations © 2009, Robin Edmonds/Beehive Illustration.

■SCHOLASTIC
www.scholastic.co.uk   **PHOTOCOPIABLE**

Inferred non-fiction clues

Objective

To identify and interpret inferred meaning from picture and text clues to better understand the author's meaning and answer inference questions.

Background knowledge

Children readily infer meaning from information once they have generated all the literal questions possible. They often do this without being aware of it. This section explains how to find inferred word and picture clues from non-fiction information and shows the children how to distinguish between being literal and inferential questioning. They need to realise that although non-fiction information is largely concerned with facts, the way it is presented to us on the page is by no means entirely literal. There is plenty that can be inferred from the text clues and photographs that suggests what is happening beyond what can be seen literally. As they learn how to locate and interpret inference clues to respond to questions, it is important that they also remember to provide evidence from the information to explain their deductions.

Skills

Explain to the children that these activities will show them how to find clues that will help them to give reasoned answers to inference questions about non-fiction information.

- **Photocopiable page 65 'Every picture tells a story'**
  - Talk with the children about the difference between being literal and using inference.
  - Explain that when they can no longer ask 'who', 'what' and 'where' questions about what they can see on the page, they need to look deeper for information that only *suggests* something – and is not obvious.

- Tell the children that these inferred clues may only hint at meaning. They will then have to make connections with other information in the picture or the text. They should also use their own knowledge to look for meaning.
- Remind the children that they always need to prove or explain how they know something.
- Hand out the photocopiable sheet and ask the children to look carefully at the picture and think about the literal 'who', 'what' and 'where' information they can see and then answer the questions.
- Once they have done this, ask them to look for clues in the picture, that might explain what is happening, and circle them.
- Ask the children to complete the questions at the bottom of the sheet. Remind them that they need to explain how they know from the clues in the picture and in the text.

Comprehension

- **Photocopiable pages 66 and 67 'Helicopter'**
  - Hand out the first photocopiable sheet and ask the children to look at the picture and read the text. Discuss the literal information in the text. Ask the children if they can work out any inferred meanings.
  - Give the children the second photocopiable sheet and ask them to answer the literal and inference questions. They will need to tick the box under PC Page's picture if the question is literal and the box under Text Detective's picture if it is an inference question.

Digital content

On the digital component you will find:
- Printable versions of all three photocopiable pages.
- Answers to 'Every picture tells a story' and 'Helicopter (2)'.
- Interactive versions of 'Every picture tells a story' and 'Helicopter'.

Inferred non-fiction clues

Every picture tells a story

The men waved back at the desperate family and radioed control to tell them that they had found five more people who needed their help. They would have to be quick. The water level was still rising.

■ Read the text and look at the picture. What questions would PC Page ask?

Who? _____

What? _____

Where? _____

■ Find and circle the inference clues in the picture and in the text that explain what is happening.

■ Why are the family waving? How do you know that?

_____

_____

_____

■ Talk to your partner about how the circled clues in the picture link to the word clues in the text. Provide evidence to support your answers to the questions above.

Illustrations © 2009, Robin Edmonds/Beehive Illustration.

Name:

Helicopter (1)

Pooleport Coastguard's brand new service was put into operation on its first day. The Augusta Westland 139 arrived in the morning and by 1400 hours it was on its way to its first emergency. It was called to a boat in Pooleport Harbour after a diver got into difficulties and stopped breathing momentarily. The man was winched aboard, flown to Pooleport and speedily transported to the hospital in the town where he received specialist treatment.

Photograph © *Sieto/www.istockphoto.com.*

PHOTOCOPIABLE

Inferred non-fiction clues

Helicopter (2)

■ Tick the PC Page box if the question is literal.
■ Tick the Text Detective box if it is an inference question.
■ Then answer the question in full.

1. Whose new service was put into operation on its first day?

_____

2. What is the Augusta Westland 139? How do you know that?

_____

_____

3. What was the helicopter being used for? Explain how you know.

_____

_____

4. When did it go to its first emergency?

_____

5. What clue tells you that the man was winched into the helicopter? Explain why you say that.

_____

_____

6. Was the man transported to hospital in a hurry when the helicopter landed? How do you know that?

_____

_____

Illustrations © 2009, Robin Edmonds/Beehive Illustration.

Seeking evidence clues

Objective

To identify inferred meaning from text clues and pictures to use as evidence to support deduction.

Background knowledge

This section builds on the skills the children have learned in the previous section. It explains how to find inferred word and picture clues from information and shows the children how to gather evidence from suggested and hidden clues to support their deductions.

It may be helpful to refer them to poster page 63 'Being a text detective' to remind them that they can delve deeper to find answers to inference questions than PC Page the literal officer who can only see what is 'right there'.

Skills

Explain to the children that these activities will show them how to find clues that enable them to give reasoned answers to inference questions about pictures and text.

● **Photocopiable page 69 'Meaning from clues'**
  ● Explain that authors and illustrators often use clues that hint at meaning within text and pictures to make their writing or pictures more interesting.
  ● The clues they introduce ask the reader to think and search for connections between the information given (key words and images) and their own knowledge to infer meaning and make deductions.
  ● Explain that when a detective infers from these clues and makes deductions he must also be able to provide evidence to prove how he knows something.

● Hand out the photocopiable sheet to the children. Ask them to look carefully at the picture and read the text searching for key information.
● Ask the children to highlight or circle any clues that they can find in the picture and in the text.
● Then ask them to link word clues with picture clues by drawing lines between them. Can they explain why these clues are linked?
● Children should then answer the questions providing evidence to support their answers and ask their own inference question.

Comprehension

● **Photocopiable pages 70 and 71 'The children who smelled a rat'**
  ● Hand out the first photocopiable sheet. Ask the children to read the text. What do they notice about the images?
  ● Provide the second photocopiable sheet and ask the children to highlight the clues in the questions before answering them. They also need to generate and answer their own questions.

Digital content

On the digital component you will find:
● Printable versions of all three photocopiable pages.
● Answers to 'Meaning from clues' and 'The children who smelled a rat (2)'.
● Interactive version of 'Meaning from clues'.

Seeking evidence clues

Meaning from clues

■ Highlight the word clues in the text and link them to clues in the picture to explain what is happening. Use these to answer the questions.

"Mum! Mum! Joey's got out! Fred's got in! Help! Quick!" shouted Tim and Rosy.

1. What happened while Mum was out of the room? How do you know that?

_____

_____

2. Is Joey in danger? How do you know that?

_____

_____

3. Your inference question:

_____

_____

Your answer:

_____

_____

Illustrations © 2009, Robin Edmonds/Beehive Illustration.

Name:

Seeking evidence clues

The children who smelled a rat (1)

Chapter 1
The Parcel

One winter's day a forgetful man

green  hat and a great  hurry left his

umbrella on a train, his  briefcase in a

bookshop, his  book – which he had only

just bought – on a park bench, and his very

important parcel  in a taxi.

Later on, much later actually, when the man came

home again, he left his  hat on his head,

forgot his  supper, and went to bed.*

Meanwhile, on that same day, it was a Friday,

Mrs Gaskitt *found* a parcel in her taxi.

And when she picked it up,

the parcel went …

Tweet!

* Which is the last we'll hear of him!

Text © 2005, Allan Ahlberg; illustrations © 2004, Katharine McEwan.

PHOTOCOPIABLE

■SCHOLASTIC
www.scholastic.co.uk

Seeking evidence clues

The children who smelled a rat (2)

1. Did the man have a poor memory most of the time? Explain why you say that.

_____

_____

_____

2. What item did the man have with him at all times throughout the day? How do you know that?

_____

_____

_____

3. What clue explains why the parcel was so special? Why do you say that?

_____

_____

_____

4. Your question:

_____

_____

Your answer: How do you know that?

_____

_____

5. Your question:

_____

_____

Your answer: How do you know that?

_____

_____

Being a text detective

Objective

To gather and present evidence that indicates a full understanding of the author's intention.

Background knowledge

Good text detectives need to offer proof that clearly explains the author's or illustrator's hidden meaning and intention. This section builds on the previous sections and shows the children how to gather and present well-reasoned evidence from information to demonstrate how or why they know the answer.

The activities in this section show them how to use the conjunction 'because' to help them link key words in the question to inferred clues from the text and picture to elicit a full evidence-based answer to an inference question. It may be helpful to refer them to Prediction Chapter 3 Section 2 that explains how links are made between cause and effect clues.

Skills

Explain to the children that these activities will show them how to link question clues and text and pictures clues to give fully justified answers to inference questions.

- **Photocopiable page 73 'A new hamster'**
  - Explain to the children that in order to give a full answer to an inference question they need to give a good reason for their answer.
  - They need to say why or how they know the answer by offering proof that explains the hidden meaning within the information they have read.
  - To do this they need to use the word 'because' to link the first part of their answer (using part of the question to guide them) to the second part that explains how they know.

- Hand out the photocopiable sheet. Talk about the question and answer example given. Discuss how the pictures and the emboldened clues are linked to give a full answer using the conjunction 'because'.
- Explain that 'because' is linked to cause and effect and is used to explain why something is happening or might happen .
- Ask them to talk about the cause and effect in the remainder of the pictures and text and to fill in 'because' on the lines provided.
- Taking note of the underlined clues in the sentences and questions, ask them to give a full answer to each question using 'because'.

Comprehension

- **Photocopiable pages 74 and 75 'I love guinea pigs'**
  - Give the children the first photocopiable sheet. Ask the children to read the text and study the pictures.
  - Hand out the second photocopiable sheet and ask the children to highlight the key word clues in the text. Tell them to give fully justified answers to the questions and generate and answer their own questions.

Digital content

On the digital component you will find:
- Printable versions of all three photocopiable pages.
- Answers to 'A new hamster' and 'I love guinea pigs (2)'.
- Interactive version of 'A new hamster'.

Being a text detective

A new hamster

■   Look at the pictures and read the text below. Use the information to answer the questions. The first one has been done for you.

because

When a new hamster is put into a box to take home they **burrow down** into the bedding to feel **safe**.

1. Why do hamsters snuggle in bedding when they are first put in a box?

Hamsters snuggle in bedding when they are first put in a box because it helps them to feel **safe**.

Avoid handling your new hamster as much as possible the first day to allow him **time to settle in**.

2. Why should you not play with hamsters when you first get them?

You should not play with hamsters when you first get them because _____

_____

Be careful not to give your hamster a **fright** when you take him out of the box or he may give you a **nip**.

3. When might a hamster bite you? How do you know?

_____

_____

Illustrations © 2009, Robin Edmonds/Beehive Illustration.

Name:

Being a text detective

I love guinea pigs (1)

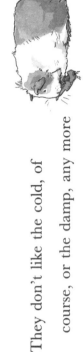

They don't like the cold, of course, or the damp, any more than you would, and they're not happy living in a poky little place, any more than you would be. But as long as they have a comfortable warm dry place to live, guinea-pigs are as happy as Larry.

Guinea-pigs like a really big roomy hutch, or, better still, a wire run out on the grass.

Guinea-pigs are such sensible animals. They're awfully easy to keep, because they aren't fussy.

PHOTOCOPIABLE

SCHOLASTIC
www.scholastic.co.uk

Text © 1994, Dick King-Smith; illustrations © 1994, Anita Jeram.

Being a text detective

I love guinea pigs (2)

1. Are guinea pigs difficult to look after? How do you know that?

_____

_____

_____

2. Should guinea pigs have a chance to exercise? What are the clues that tell you?

_____

_____

_____

3. Do guinea pigs enjoy the winter months? How do you know that?

_____

_____

_____

4. Your question:

_____

Your answer: How do you know that?

_____

_____

5. Your question:

_____

Your answer: How do you know that?

_____

_____

Asking and answering inference questions

Objective

To gather, organise and classify inferred information to formulate questions and answers from text and pictures.

Background knowledge

The skills in this section show the children how to gather and organise complex inference clues to generate their own questions and answers from text. These are invaluable skills that will help them to demonstrate an understanding of the author's intention from several perspectives. With practice they will soon be able to question and respond by making links with a variety of clues in different parts of the text. They will see for themselves how there is often more than one correct answer to an inference question. As long as the evidence presented justifies the answer to a question, then it is acceptable. These essential skills encourage the children to think for themselves and help them to investigate and question, make reasoned deductions and present evidence with confidence that impacts on their learning across the curriculum.

Skills

These activities will show the children how to find inference clues that will help them to ask and answer their own questions about stories or non-fiction.

● **Photocopiable page 77 'Creature of the lake'**
  ● Remind the children that inference questions ask readers to solve clues from information that is suggested in the text. Sometimes clues that justify the answer to a question clue are found in different parts of the text.

● Hand out the photocopiable sheet. Read the passage to the children. Ask them to listen out for clues that imply something, for example: *lone walkers* (not more than one person at a time), *some say/others say* (not everyone agrees).

● Ask them to circle key word clues given on the page and search for other implied words and phrases. Can they find other words in the text with meaning that is associated with these clues? For example: *huge jaws/could eat an elephant, lurks alone/shy*.

● Tell the children to read the question examples. Talk about the answers to these questions and how the clues link the question to the text. Show how the first question on the page checks the readers' understanding of the text.

● Ask them to generate their own questions from clues in the text.

● When they give evidence to show how they know, it helps to quote directly from the text.

Comprehension

● **Photocopiable pages 78 and 79 'The sea monster'**
  ● Hand out the first photocopiable sheet. Ask the children to highlight the key information in the text and picture.
  ● Give them the second photocopiable sheet and ask them to answer the two questions and finally generate and answer their own questions.

Digital content

On the digital component you will find:
● Printable versions of all three photocopiable pages.
● Answers to 'Creature of the lake' and 'The sea monster (2)'.
● Interactive version of 'Creature of the lake'.

Asking and answering inference questions

Creature of the lake

Very few people have ever seen it. Early in the morning, on a quiet day, a few lone walkers and fishermen have reported sightings of a 'monstrous creature' by the lakeside.

Some say it looks like a gigantic silver-green snake that is at least 80 feet long! Others have reported that it has a small head with triangular ears and a **cavernous mouth** that looks as if it could **eat an elephant**! It is generally believed that the monster has short legs and moves quite slowly on the land. But in the lake it's a different matter – it moves faster than a speedboat, zooming through the water ready to snatch up fish – or other living things – with its **huge jaws**.

Many people believe that it is a very shy creature that lurks alone in the deep waters. Through the **busy summer months** the **sightings stop**. Locals believe that it stays hidden waiting for the tourists to go before it ventures ashore again.

Key word clues from text:			
busy summer months	shy	lurks alone in the deep waters	tourists

Example: What **time of the year** are you most unlikely to see the monster? How do you know that? The time of year that you are most unlikely to see the monster is over the 'busy summer months' because it says the sightings stop.

Key word clues from text:			
monster	cavernous mouth	huge jaws	eat an elephant

Does the monster **have a** small mouth**? How do you know that?**

_____

_____

■ Look for more key word clues from the text to ask and answer your own inference question. Remember to also ask 'How do you know that?' and answer 'because'.

Illustrations © 2009, Robin Edmonds/Beehive Illustration.

Name:

Asking and answering inference questions

The sea monster (1)

High on the cliff above the corner of the beach, in a grey stone cottage, there lived an old fisherman. It was a while since he had sailed the seas catching fish and most of the time now he made model boats…

…or sat alone on the cliff top watching the boats sail by. He saw seals and porpoises and great basking sharks, and sometimes he saw strange green lights shining in the murky deep. On this morning he heard barking in the bay below and, looking down, saw a little white dog jumping from rock to rock and splashing in the surf. Turning to the ocean, the old fisherman could just make out the head of a boy among the distant waves.

Text and illustrations © 2005, Chris Wormell.

PHOTOCOPIABLE

SCHOLASTIC
www.scholastic.co.uk

The sea monster (2)

while since	catch fish	most of time now	made model boats

1. How was life different for the fisherman in his old age? How do you know that?

_____

_____

_____

high	cliff	corner of beach	grey stone	cottage

2. Did the old fisherman live in a wooden shack on the beach? Explain how you know.

_____

_____

_____

3. Your inference question:

_____

Your answer:

_____

_____

4. Your inference question:

_____

Your answer:

_____

_____

Chapter 5

Clarification

Introduction

This chapter helps children make sense of what they read by showing them how to resolve difficulties with unfamiliar words, images and concepts by combining prior knowledge and contextual clues. For children to gain contextual understanding of language they need to be taught explicitly how to interpret the meaning of words in context.

Children will also learn to identify synonyms and antonyms and practice skimming and scanning information for clues to ask and answer questions. For further practice, please see the 'Clarification' section in the Year 4 workbook.

Poster notes

The text patrol (page 81)
This poster shows how prior knowledge and context clues helps children to make sense of unknown words. It shows them how to isolate what they know of a difficult word and fathom its meaning from their understanding of the words around it. They are shown how PC Code-Breaker solves difficult words by gaining the 'gist' of the author's meaning, breaking the difficult word down into small parts and finally checking that the meaning 'fits' the sentence and the context of the passage.

In this chapter

	About each section	About the comprehension activity
What does it mean? page 82	Children look inside unknown words to reveal their meaning.	Children look for clues that explain how traditional pizzas are cooked.
Similar and opposite meanings page 86	Children identify synonyms and antonyms to gain understanding.	Children answer questions about *Flabby Cat and Slobby Dog* by Jeanne Willis and Tony Ross, using similar and opposite meanings.
Skimming and scanning page 90	Children are introduced to skimming and scanning to find key words in text and pictures.	Children match key words in text with same words in questions about *Dr Xargle's Earth Tiggers* by Jeanne Willis to give accurate answers.
Synonyms and antonyms page 94	Children build on skimming and scanning technique to link synonym or antonym key clues in text and questions.	Children skim and scan for synonyms and antonyms to answer questions on *Why do we look like our parents?* by Elspeth Graham.

Clarification

The text patrol

Let me
show you what to do
If you're stuck on a word that's new...
Break up the word – what does it show?
It may be a small word you already know.
The first part of a word often gives a clue
To the meaning of the whole word –
Using the context too.

My job is to patrol the text and figure out the words I don't understand.

Sometimes you can read a word – but you don't know what it means.

If you get stuck... go back to the beginning of the sentence. Read again.

You can... leave the word out and read on to the end of the sentence.

Then... break the word up. You might get an idea of the meaning of the whole word from the first part, for example: human (ism), quarter (ly), grim (ace). Read on to the end of the sentence.

Now ask yourself... Does the meaning you are thinking of make sense within the sentence? Does it fit the context of the paragraph?

Finally check the word... Ask a friend, your teacher or look it up in a dictionary... Are you right? Yes, you are a brilliant code-breaker!

PC Code-Breaker

Illustrations © 2009, Robin Edmonds/Beehive Illustration.

What does it mean?

Objective

To make sense of unfamiliar words and images using contextual clues and what you know already.

Background knowledge

This section shows the children how to solve unknown words to support their understanding of text. Non-fiction often contains specialist words that are new to children. Although these words may at first appear strange, when they are broken down into parts (morphemes) they often reveal smaller, more familiar words and meaning. For example: 'pizzer–ria'. Other words, such as compound words (single words joined together) such as 'takeaway', may also appear unfamiliar till separated. These small units of meaning help children to see links to the subject matter and often enable them to predict the meaning of the whole word correctly. However, when the children predict the meaning of a word, they must also check it makes sense within context, before reading on. These skills help children to combine their prior knowledge, prediction and interpretation skills to make sense out of confusion as they read.

Skills

Explain to the children that these activities will help them to focus on meaning and sense within context and ask them to justify their solutions.

- **Photocopiable page 83 'What do they mean?'**
  - Tell the children that to fully understand what they are reading, they need to clarify meanings as they go along.

- Explain that although some non-fiction words may look difficult and unfamiliar, once they are broken into parts they often reveal a smaller word they know, such as 'human–itarian'. Compound words (two words linked together), such as 'pipeline', may also be more easily understood if looked at separately. Tell the children that the parts of a word often uncover the meaning of the whole word as soon as they are linked to clues in the context of the passage.
- Hand out the photocopiable sheet. Ask the children to break the words into two parts. Can they see small word(s) that makes sense to them within the parts? Ask them to then talk about the meaning of the images in connection with these words. Can they guess the meaning of the whole word from these clues?
- Ask them to write the word that fits the context of the sentences in the space provided. Remind them to check they make sense.
- Tell them to discuss and predict the meaning of the compound words in groups. Then write a sentence that shows they understand the meaning of each one.

Comprehension

- **Photocopiable pages 84 and 85 'Italian pizzeria'**
  - Hand out the photocopiable sheets. Ask the children to look at the photograph and explain what is happening.
  - Then ask them to answer the questions and generate and answer their own question.

Digital content

On the digital component you will find:
- Printable versions of all three photocopiable pages.
- Answers to 'What do they mean?' and 'Italian pizzeria (2)'.
- Interactive version of 'What do they mean?'

What does it mean?

What do they mean?

■ Break the words into two parts to find the meaning that links them to the picture clues. Can you define them?

grimace   seascape   quarterly   humanitarian

■ Use the context to complete the sentences using the words above. Check if the word makes sense in the context.

1. She cares about human welfare. She is a _____

2. My mum pays the bills every quarter of the year. They are _____ payments.

3. The clown looked grim as he 'pulled a funny face'. He likes to _____ at people to make them laugh.

4. One look and it is like I'm at the seaside. My grandfather has a _____ painting that hangs on his sitting room wall.

■ Look at the words below. Can you work out the meanings of the compound words? Use the pictures to help you. Write some sentences to explain the meanings of each one.

newscaster   earthenware   runway   pipeline   crosscheck

Illustrations © 2009, Robin Edmonds/Beehive Illustration.

SCHOLASTIC
www.scholastic.co.uk   **PHOTOCOPIABLE**   **Scholastic English Skills**
Comprehension: Year 4   **83**

Name:

What does it mean?

Italian pizzeria (1)

Many Italian pizzerias still use traditional wood-burning ovens. The hot embers are pushed to one side and then the pizza is slipped off the pizza paddle (or peel) straight onto the oven floor.

The smell of an oven-baked pizza is mouth-watering!

This is the best takeaway food!

Photograph: JupiterImages.

PHOTOCOPIABLE

■SCHOLASTIC
www.scholastic.co.uk

What does it mean?

Italian pizzeria (2)

1. Circle the compound word in the text (two words joined together) and explain in a sentence what it means.

_____

_____

_____

2. Explain what you think a 'pizzeria' is. Why do you say that?

_____

_____

_____

3. Why do you think the 'pizza paddle' was given its name?

_____

_____

_____

4. Why do you think the Italian pizzerias produce the 'best takeaway food'?

_____

_____

_____

5. Your clarification question:

_____

_____

Your answer:

_____

_____

Similar and opposite meanings

Objective

To make sense of contextual clues that have similar and opposite meanings.

Background knowledge

Showing children how to use synonyms and antonyms is an excellent way of preparing them for text detective work. As they practise collecting words that have a similar meaning to other words it enables them to build their knowledge and understanding of vocabulary significantly. They are then able to use this knowledge to ask inference questions and to classify words and make links with this information to answer them. They learn to locate contextual clues and identify and apply inferred meaning.

Synonyms and antonyms are often presented as clues in inference questions. A synonym can often replace another word without affecting the meaning or sense of the context, for example 'small' can replace 'tiny'. Antonyms are often used to test the readers' interpretation and understanding of a word by suggesting the opposite meaning of the word used in the text.

Skills

Explain to the children that these activities will help them to identify and classify words that have similar and opposite meanings.

- **Photocopiable page 87 'Webs and pairs'**
  - Tell the children that a brilliant text detective needs to have a good knowledge and understanding of words with similar or opposite meanings.

- Explain to the children that inference questions often contain word clues such as synonyms (words with similar meanings) and antonyms (words that have opposite meanings). An answer can often be found in the text (or perhaps in an illustration) by searching for a word (or image) that has a similar meaning to a word in the question. For example: *Is the witch bad? Yes because it says 'the evil witch laughed'*.
- Sometimes an answer can be found by searching for a word that has an opposite meaning. For example: *Is the witch kind? No, because it says that the 'witch is mean'*.
- Hand out the photocopiable sheet and talk through the similar and opposite word examples given. Then ask the children to complete the sheet.
- The children can then be challenged to make their own lists of antonyms or synonyms.

Comprehension

- **Photocopiable pages 88 and 89 'Flabby Cat and Slobby Dog'**
  - Hand out the photocopiable sheets and ask the children to read the text and look at the picture.
  - Ask them to read the questions and search the text for words with similar or opposite meanings to those in the questions. They should then answer the questions and generate and answer their own question.

Digital content

On the digital component you will find:
- Printable versions of all three photocopiable pages.
- Answers to 'Webs and pairs' and 'Flabby Cat and Slobby Dog (2)'.
- Interactive version of 'Webs and pairs'.

Similar and opposite meanings

Webs and pairs

■ Write a word in each section of the web that has a similar meaning to the word in the web centre.

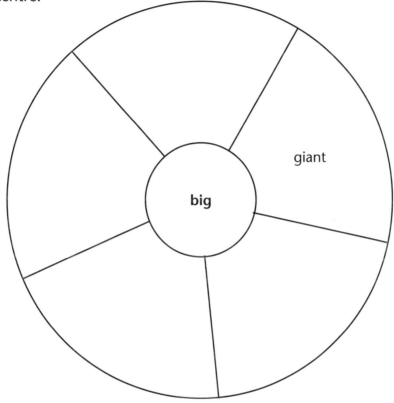

■ Match the word which has the opposite meaning. Draw a line between them.

before	miserable
cheerful	beginning
awake	after
end	asleep

SCHOLASTIC
www.scholastic.co.uk   **PHOTOCOPIABLE**

Name:

Flabby Cat and Slobby Dog (1)

Flabby Cat was sitting on the sofa when in came Slobby Dog.

He sat next to her like he'd always done since they were small.

But today, they just couldn't get comfortable.

"I'm all squashed," said Slobby Dog. "This sofa has shrunk."

"Nonsense!" said Flabby Cat. "The cushions have grown."

"That's it," said Slobby Dog.

"It's very uncomfortable. Whatever shall we do?" said Flabby Cat

"Let's do what we always do," said Slobby Dog.

Text © 2009, Jeanne Willis; illustrations © 2009, Tony Ross.

PHOTOCOPIABLE ◾**SCHOLASTIC**
www.scholastic.co.uk

Similar and opposite meanings

Flabby Cat and Slobby Dog (2)

Example of a question using a synonym clue:

Question: Had Slobby Dog sat with Flabby Cat before? Explain how you know that.

Answer: Yes, Slobby Dog has sat with Flabby Cat before because it says 'he sat next to her like he'd always done'.

1. Were Slobby Dog and Flabby Cat old friends? How do you know that?

2. Did Slobby Dog think the sofa was larger than normal? What evidence do you have for saying that?

3. Did Slobby Dog's comments about the sofa make sense to Flabby Cat? How do you know that?

4. Your question (using a synonym or antonym):

Your answer:

Skimming and scanning

Objective

To answer literal questions from text by skimming and scanning to locate the same words as the key words that appear in the question.

Background knowledge

Skimming is used to quickly identify the main ideas of a text and scanning involves searching for key words and ideas within a long passage and illustration. These skills help children to answer literal questions with accuracy, confidence and speed, and prepare them for more complex inference and evaluation questions later on.

To answer a literal question successfully they need only locate the key word in the question, then search for the same word and meaning in the text. They can do this quickly if they learn to skim text from left to right, scan up and down, and follow these tips:

- Repeat the word in your head.
- Look for the starting letter.
- Focus on the shape and length of the word you are looking for to find the matching word in the text.
- Finally, highlight the key words in the question and in the text as you locate them.

Skills

This activity will show the children how to find matching key words in text quickly to help them find the answers to literal questions accurately and swiftly.

- **Photocopiable page 91 'Skim and scan for the word'**
  - Tell the children that to answer literal questions from text easily and accurately they need to practise skimming and scanning skills.

- Explain that these skills will help them to match the key words in the questions with the same words in the text and lead them to the answer.
- Hand out the photocopiable sheet. Ask pairs or small groups to read the clues, write the answers on the lines and then to locate and circle the answer to the clues given from the list of words in the box.
- Now racing against the clock, ask them to search the puzzle for the words they have circled. Remind them to skim left to right and scan up and down to find them. Tell them to say the word they are looking for in their heads, to look for the initial letter and remember the shape and length of the word.
- Remind them that the information they are looking for is there on the page and that they may find it helpful to highlight the words as they find them.

Comprehension

- **Photocopiable pages 92 and 93 'Earth Tiggers'**
  - Hand out the first photocopiable sheet. Discuss the picture and text with the children.
  - Give them the second photocopiable sheet and ask them to skim and scan for the main ideas and key words to answer the questions and formulate their own questions and answers.

Digital content

On the digital component you will find:
- Printable versions of all three photocopiable pages.
- Answers to 'Skim and scan for the word' and 'Earth Tiggers (2)'.
- Interactive versions of 'Skim and scan for the word' and 'Earth Tiggers'.

Skimming and scanning

Skim and scan for the word

■ Complete the clues using the words in the box. Then skim and scan for the answers in the word search.

1. A water animal that has a shell. _____

2. Hair on the upper lip. _____

3. Something you write with. _____

4. A brief fall of rain. _____

5. A part of your face. _____

6. Direct information – right there on the page. _____

7. Asking to find out something. _____

8. Someone who makes things out of clay. _____

9. Opposite meaning of quiet. _____

10. Writer of a book. _____

p	s	o	g	x	z	y	w	a	o
e	q	u	e	s	t	i	o	n	p
n	c	c	u	e	l	s	o	b	p
m	o	u	s	t	a	c	h	e	o
s	h	e	l	l	f	i	s	h	t
e	k	c	h	i	n	x	b	t	t
a	u	t	h	o	r	y	i	i	e
s	h	o	w	e	r	j	f	g	r
q	i	m	l	i	t	e	r	a	l
r	n	o	i	s	y	p	n	c	z

Word box:
- pen
- literal
- moustache
- noisy
- shellfish
- author
- question
- potter
- shower
- chin

Name:

Earth Tiggers (1)

A healthy Earth Tigger also needs cowjuice, tandoori cluck bird, muckworm and old green gibble in dustbin gravy.

Text © 1990, Jeanne Willis; Illustration © 1990, Tony Ross.

PHOTOCOPIABLE

Skimming and scanning

Earth Tiggers (2)

1. What are the creatures in the picture called?

    _____

2. What are they rummaging around inside?

    _____

3. What sort of juice does a healthy Earth Tigger need?

    _____

4. What is in dustbin gravy?

    _____

5. What is the cat doing on top of the dustbin?

    _____

6. Your question:

    _____

    _____

    Your answer:

    _____

    _____

7. Your question:

    _____

    _____

    Your answer:

    _____

Synonyms and antonyms

Objectives

To learn how to skim and scan for similar and opposite meanings within text and pictures that link to question key clues. To infer from these clues to answer questions and support deduction.

Background knowledge

This section builds on the previous section and shows children how to search for word clues that have similar or opposite meanings to key words in the questions. Skimming and scanning for these clues enables children to answer and generate their own inference questions with greater ease. Searching for and identifying synonyms and antonyms also helps to enlarge their understanding of word meanings within context; extends their vocabulary and stimulates prediction and deduction. These activities show the children how to locate key words in a question and how to find words that suggest a similar or opposite meaning on the page. They learn how to gather this information to respond to questions accurately and appropriately.

Skills

These activities show the children how to answer inference questions accurately by finding similar and opposite key clues in text and images to match the word clues in the questions.

- **Photocopiable page 95 'Crying Jack'**
  - Explain that many inference questions need you to skim and scan information for similar and opposite meanings to answer word clues in the questions.
  - Hand out the photocopiable sheet. Read the poem with the children and discuss the vocabulary within the pictures and text. Ask them to locate the word in the poem that is represented by a picture.

- Ask them to re-read the poem in pairs and to think about each of the emboldened words in context. *What other word would make sense in place of each word?*
- Tell them to look at the first list of words. Each link to words in the text.
- Ask them to skim and scan the text and using coloured pens circle the words that are similar in meaning to the words listed – explaining why to their partner.
- Ask them to repeat this exercise with the following list of words. They must focus on the 'opposite' meanings to the words listed and circle them in a different coloured pen.
- Finally ask them to read the questions at the bottom of the page and answer them using the circled words in the text to help them.

Comprehension

- **Photocopiable pages 96 and 97 'Why do we look like our parents?'**
  - Hand out the first photocopiable sheet. Ask the children to read the text carefully.
  - Give the children the second photocopiable sheet. The children need to identify vocabulary and meaning in the text, and highlight the question key words that link to similar and opposite words in the text before answering the questions. They also need to generate and answer their own question.

Digital content

On the digital component you will find:
- Printable versions of all three photocopiable pages.
- Answers to 'Crying Jack' and 'Why do we look like our parents? (2)'
- Interactive versions of 'Crying Jack' and 'Why do we look like our parents?'

Synonyms and antonyms

Crying Jack

Once a little boy, Jack, was, oh! Ever so **good**,

Till he took the **bad** notion to cry all he could.

So he **cried** all the day, and he cried all the night,

He cried in the morning and in the twilight;

He cried till his voice was as **hoarse** as a crow,

And his mouth grew so **large** it looked like a great O.

It grew at the **bottom** and grew at the top;

It grew till they thought that it never would stop.

Each day his great mouth grew taller and taller,

And his dear little self grew **shorter** and shorter.

At last, that same mouth grew so big that – alack! –

It was only a mouth with a border of Jack.

■ Skim and scan the text to find synonyms (similar words) to the following:

awful   wept   big   gruff   base   smaller

■ Skim and scan the text to find antonyms (opposite words) to the following:

evening   longer   laughed   start

■ Answer these questions.

1. Did Jack weep until his voice became gruff? How do you know that?

2. Did he cry only in the morning? Explain why you say that.

3. Explain why Jack's mouth looked like a huge 'O' shape.

4. What happened to Jack in the end because he sobbed so much?

Illustrations © 2009, Robin Edmonds/Beehive Illustration.

SCHOLASTIC
www.scholastic.co.uk   **PHOTOCOPIABLE**   **Scholastic English Skills**
Comprehension: Year 4   **95**

Name:

Why do we look like our parents? (1)

When there is a new baby in the family everyone begins to say things like: 'Isn't he just like his dad; he's got those same big blue eyes, he's got his long fingers, he has his dark curly hair.' Or: 'Isn't she like her mum; she has her mum's tiny nose and her little shell-like ears and look at those stubby toes…'

It is true – we are often like our parents or even our grandparents. You may have your grandfather's strong muscles or your grandmother's wonderful voice. We are like them.

The important thing that decides what we look like is called DNA.

DNA is made up of a long chain of molecules. This chain makes up a coded message. The order of the molecules in the chain tells the body how it should look: tall, short, dark, fair, slender, stocky and so on.

DNA comes from our parents – we have copies of their DNA – one chain from each parent. That's why we look similar to them. We're not exact copies. If your dad has curly hair and your mum has straight hair then only one of these features can win. One parent's code must win and the other parent's code must lose. This is why we're all different – all unique.

Photograph © 2007 Bananastock.

PHOTOCOPIABLE

Synonyms and antonyms

Why do we look like our parents? (2)

1. Read the passage. Find a word that has a similar meaning to these words and write it next to it.

    small _____   frequent _____

    thin _____

2. Read the passage then write a word from it that means the opposite to these words in the text.

    weak _____   straight _____

    different _____

3. Is it a fact that we may not only look like our parents but also look like our grandparents?

    _____

    _____

4. Do people talk about how similar we look to our parents when we are born? Explain why you say this.

    _____

    _____

5. Is DNA made up of a single molecule? How do you know?

    _____

    _____

6. Your question (using a synonym or antonym):

    _____

    _____

    Your answer:

    _____

SCHOLASTIC
www.scholastic.co.uk   **PHOTOCOPIABLE**   Scholastic English Skills
Comprehension: Year 4   **97**

Chapter 6

Evaluation

Introduction

Evaluation refers here to personal interpretation of story characters that links to the author's viewpoint, rather than the term that is generally used to mean a critical appraisal of text by the reader. It is generally a question type that children enjoy because it asks them to explain what they think the characters' feelings, thoughts and actions might be based on their own experience and understanding of the world. They also like evaluation questions because as long as they justify their answers from the text and pictures, any answer is valid. In addition, evaluation questioning develops empathy and evidence-based reasoning to support personal opinion and debate. For further practice, please see the 'Evaluation' section in the Year 4 workbook.

Poster notes

Are you a private detective? (page 99)
Private detectives make meaning of words and images by using a combination of all the comprehension skills: literal, prediction, clarification and inference. This poster supports children's understanding of evaluation and introduces them to the Private Detectives who are the highest ranking officers of the 'Literacy Force'. Reference to 'Private' reminds the children that evaluation detective-work also asks them to add personal experiences and knowledge.

   The poster is a useful classroom aid that shows the children how they need to work with all the comprehension characters to be Private Detectives and best friends with the author.

In this chapter

	About each section	About the comprehension activity
Characters' feelings and actions page 100	Children interpret facial expressions and body language.	Children answer questions about the players in a football photograph.
What you think page 104	Children use personal experiences and evidence from words and images to support evaluative reasoning.	Children consider the difference between literal, inference and evaluation using an extract from *The dragon snatcher* by MP Robertson.
Characters' thoughts page 108	Children identify evaluation clues and linking clues about characters' feelings, actions and intentions to understand their thinking.	Children use their own experience to ask and answer questions using a passage from *Billy the kid* by Michael Morpurgo.
Evaluation questions page 112	Children link key evaluative words in text and pictures to ask and answer questions.	Children make links between the clues in the questions and text to answer questions about *The war and Freddy* by Dennis Hamley.

Evaluation

Are you a private detective?

> We tell you what we think is happening and **why** from our own experience and from the evidence on the page…

Private Detectives

We are private detectives – we're the best,
We add our own skills to all the rest.
We search for clues that make the link
With how characters feel and what they think.

Illustrations © 2009, Robin Edmonds/Beehive Illustration.

SCHOLASTIC
www.scholastic.co.uk   **PHOTOCOPIABLE**

Characters' feelings and actions

To draw on personal experience to interpret characters' emotions and actions within pictures and text to explain what is happening or may happen next.

Background knowledge

Evaluation questioning requires the children to put on their Private Detective hats and ask themselves: *What do I think about the characters' feelings and actions in relation to my own experience?* It asks them to uncover evidence to explain the characters' behaviour, and unfolding events in the story. The use of visual imagery draws powerful evaluation responses from children, especially when it mirrors their personal world. Children are particularly able to identify with the characters when facial expressions and body language are explicit in the picture. The emotions they express prompt children's empathy and invite them to make links to other clues on the page, to deduce what is happening and what may happen next in the story.

Skills

These activities help the children to recognise and interpret facial expressions and body language to explain the thinking and behaviour of characters within picture narrative.

- **Photocopiable page 101 'Feelings and actions'**
  - Ask the children to explain how they know when someone is feeling happy, sad, angry and so on.
  - Talk with them about how our facial expressions and behaviour communicate our feelings and thoughts to others.

- Explain that facial expressions and body language do not generally need words for us to understand and predict what people are feeling or why they are behaving in a certain way. We all recognise and share the emotions behind these expressions from time to time.
- Hand out the photocopiable sheet. Ask the children to look closely at the four picture boxes. Explain that each box contains a scene where the characters' feelings and emotions are described by their body language and facial expressions.
- Ask the children in pairs to discuss the pictures and locate the clues that explain what the characters might be thinking and feeling.
- Then, using the picture clues they have found, ask them to say what they think is happening and what may happen next in the scene.

Comprehension

- **Photocopiable pages 102 and 103 'Red card'**
  - Show the children the photograph from the first photocopiable sheet. Ask the children to explain what is happening in the picture.
  - Hand out the photocopiable sheets and ask the children to answer the evaluation questions. Remind the children that there is no wrong answer for an evaluation question – as long as their explanations refer to the picture and text as well as their own experience and knowledge. They also need to generate and answer their own questions.

Digital content

On the digital component you will find:
- Printable versions of all three photocopiable pages.
- Answers to 'Red card (2)'.
- Interactive versions of 'Feelings and actions' and 'Red card'.

Characters' feelings and actions

Feelings and actions

■ Look at the four picture boxes below. What does the body language and expression on the faces tell you about how they are feeling and what might happen next?

Illustrations © 2009, Robin Edmonds/Beehive Illustration.

Name:

Characters' feelings and actions

Red card (1)

Photograph © 2007 Image Source/JupiterImages.

PHOTOCOPIABLE   ■ SCHOLASTIC
www.scholastic.co.uk

Characters' feelings and actions

Red card (2)

1. Explain what you think is happening in the photo scene. Why do you say that?

_____

_____

2. Why do you think the player is holding back the other player? Why do you say that?

_____

_____

3. What do you think would happen if the player didn't hold his teammate back? Give your reason for saying this.

_____

_____

4. How do you think the referee is feeling? Why do you say that?

_____

_____

5. Your 'do you think' question:

_____

Your answer:

_____

6. Your 'do you think' question:

_____

Your answer:

_____

■SCHOLASTIC   **PHOTOCOPIABLE**
www.scholastic.co.uk

What you think

Objective

To understand that an evaluation question asks you to use your literal and inference skills, and personal experience to think about a character's feelings or actions.

Background knowledge

Pictures are a rich source of visual literal, inferential and evaluative information. Working with images helps teachers to show the children how to 'see' the different layers of literal meaning, the suggested meaning of inference and the more personal meaning of evaluation.

To enable children to more easily identify evaluation clues it is helpful for them to first talk through what they can literally see is happening on the page. Then look more closely for clues that hint at the possible problems and outcomes. Finally they need to look at the characters' expressions and body language in the picture and ask themselves what they think the characters might be thinking or feeling. This reference to their own experiences and prior knowledge helps them to identify with the characters and make sense of the events in the scene.

Skills

These activities help the children to recognise evaluation and to see the difference between literal, inference and evaluation clues and evidence within picture narrative.

- **Photocopiable page 105 'Looking for different clues'**
    - Begin by asking the children to explain the differences between literal PC Page and the inference Text Detective.
    - Revisit poster page 63 'Being a text detective' and discuss how he searches for evidence beyond the obvious 'who', 'what' and 'where' information to show how he uncovers the author's meaning.

- Then, using poster page 99 'Are you a private detective?', show the children how they are able to add to the Text Detective's evidence by using their own personal experience to explain what might be happening from the characters' perspective.
- Hand out the photocopiable sheet. Ask them to look at the pictures, read the captions and in pairs talk about the picture contents.
- Explain that each picture reveals particular information for PC Page, the Text Detective and the Private Detectives to ask and answer questions from.
- Explain that pictures one and two give examples of literal and inference clues that link to the word clues in the caption. Ask the children to circle and link these clues.
- Next, ask them to circle the evaluation clues in picture three and the caption that indicate the characters' feelings and thoughts.
- Ask them how the clues they have circled are different from the inference clues.

Comprehension

- **Photocopiable pages 106 and 107 'The dragon snatcher'**
    - Hand out the photocopiable sheets to the children. Ask the children to read the text and look at the picture.
    - Ask them to answer the questions. Remind the children of the difference between question types to answer them correctly and that evaluation answers must refer to picture and text as well as personal experience. They also need to generate and answer their own questions.

Digital content

On the digital component you will find:
- Printable versions of all three photocopiable pages.
- Answers to 'The dragon snatcher (2)'.
- Interactive version of 'The dragon snatcher'.

Name:

Looking for different clues

■ Circle clues in the pictures and text to help PC Page, the Text Detective and the Private Detectives gather literal, inference and evaluation information.

PC Page:
Who? What? Where?
Right there!

The Text Detective:
searching for clues and evidence that suggests what is happening and what might happen next.

Private Detectives:
finding evidence to back up what you think the characters are feeling and thinking.

The boy is looking through the hedge.

The collie dog was gaining on them, the farmer wouldn't be far behind.

As soon as he felt the hand on his shoulder he knew they were in real trouble. He felt embarrassed, angry at the others and didn't know what they were going to say.

Illustrations © 2009, Robin Edmonds/Beehive Illustration.

■ SCHOLASTIC
www.scholastic.co.uk

PHOTOCOPIABLE

The dragon snatcher (1)

George peered out of his window. Looking up at him was his dragon. He had a worried look in his yellow eye. George threw a blanket around his shoulders and climbed out on to the dragon's neck. He clung tightly as they were whisked on the North Wind to a land that was neither Here nor There.

Text and illustrations © 2005, M P Robertson.

What you think

The dragon snatcher (2)

1. Who peered out of his window?

   _____

2. Was the dragon feeling anxious? How do you know that?

   _____

   _____

3. Do you think George is frightened of the dragon? Why do you say that?

   _____

   _____

4. Are George and the dragon good friends? Explain why you think that.

   _____

   _____

5. What do you think George was feeling as the dragon flew off into the sky? Give your reason for saying this.

   _____

   _____

6. Your literal question:

   _____

   Your answer:

   _____

7. Your inference question:

   _____

   Your answer:

   _____

8. Your evaluation question:

   _____

   Your answer:

   _____

Characters' thoughts

Objective

To identify characters' thoughts, feelings and reactions to changing events from word clues to support understanding of evaluation within text.

Background knowledge

Once children are able to identify evaluation concepts within text and pictures and understand the difference between literal, inferential and evaluative meaning, it is important for them to be able to locate evaluation word clues that indicate how the character is feeling, thinking and behaving. When they can justify characters' feelings and their reactions to changing events in a narrative, they will be able to answer and generate these questions with ease. This section helps them to achieve this by asking them to firstly locate words from the text that they associate with emotions and reactions; secondly interpret these thoughts and actions by using their own personal experiences to explain the individual's feelings and responses to the changing events in the text; and lastly say why they think these changes have taken place from the clues they have gathered.

Skills

These activities will help the children to give reasons for characters' actions, thoughts or feelings using their own experience and evidence from the text to ask and answer questions.

- **Photocopiable page 109 'Fido'**
  - Explain that the children are going to be shown how to locate evaluation information from text that: firstly focuses on the emotional events and situations; then asks them to find word clues that link to the characters' thoughts, feelings and actions to explain their reaction to the changes in the story.

- Hand out the photocopiable sheet. Ask the children to read the passage in pairs, talk about the events in the story and list them on a separate sheet of paper, for example: *Fido's birth, Boxing Day, growing up* and *death*.
- Tell them to skim and scan the text for the literal 'who', 'what' and 'where' information for each heading. Then look for clues that suggest what the characters may have been thinking and feeling during these events and write them down.
- Ask the children to draw a timeline of events from the story for example: from 'Choosing Fido' to 'Fido's death'. The children may find it useful to use the key event information listed.
- From the information they have gathered, ask them to list the changes that happen throughout the story.
- Talk as a class about how the events and characters' feelings and emotions changed and why.
- Ask them to answer the questions at the bottom of the page.

Comprehension

- **Photocopiable pages 110 and 111 'Billy the kid'**
  - Give the children both photocopiable sheets. Ask them to read the text first and study the image.
  - Remind them that their personal experiences and evidence from the text will be needed to support evaluative reasoning when answering the questions and generating their own questions.

Digital content

On the digital component you will find:
- Printable versions of all three photocopiable pages.
- Answers to 'Fido' and 'Billy the kid (2)'.

Characters' thoughts

Fido

Fido died on his birthday. I remember it was his birthday because he was born on Boxing Day and Aunty Jane and Uncle Tom stayed an extra day (which they never normally did) just to see the puppies arrive.

Mum gave me the choice of one from the litter. I thought I didn't care much for dogs, but as soon as I saw him I knew there was something special about him. He was the one that wriggled the most and climbed all over the others to get to his mother's milk first. He always loved his food!

Then as we grew up together he filled my days with ball games, long walks and play-fights in the garden. He was my best friend – all I needed.

We buried him with his ball and food bowl under the apple tree where we had played. Aunty Jane and Uncle Tom stayed especially to say goodbye and they have stayed every Boxing Day since. I promised Fido I'd never have another dog and I don't play ball or go for long walks any more.

■ List the key events which happen in the story. Create a timeline using the information in the text.

■ Answer these questions.

1. Why do you think Aunty Jane and Uncle Tom stayed every Boxing Day after Fido died?

2. Why do you think the main character changed his mind about dogs and became such good friends with his pup?

3. How do you think all the family felt when Fido died? Why do you say that?

Illustrations © 2009, Robin Edmonds/Beehive Illustration.

Name:

Characters' thoughts

Billy the kid (1)

Only a few days after I scored that first goal out there in the park, my dad died. Suddenly there was no more coughing in the house. Mum let me carry his football to his funeral. I held her hand all the way through. For the first time it was me holding her hand, not the other way round. We buried him in Putney churchyard, down by the river. It was a grey day. He always loved the river. We'd often go feeding the ducks down there, then we'd sit and watch the boats go chugging by. So it was just the right place for him. You've got to be in the right place when you're dead, that's what I think. I mean, after all, you're dead for a long time, aren't you? I greased the football up when I got back home and put it back up on the shelf in the kitchen, and that's where it stayed. I never kicked it again after that.

Text © 2000, Michael Morpurgo; illustration © 2000, Michael Foreman.

PHOTOCOPIABLE

SCHOLASTIC
www.scholastic.co.uk

Characters' thoughts

Billy the kid (2)

1. Do you think Billy will always be reminded of his dad when he plays football? Why do you say that?

_____

_____

2. How do you think Billy felt about his mum after his dad died? Explain why you say that.

_____

_____

3. How do you think life changed for Billy after his dad had died? What evidence do you have for saying that?

_____

_____

4. What do you think Billy felt about his dad's funeral? Why do you say that?

_____

_____

5. Your question:

_____

_____

Your answer:

_____

_____

6. Your question:

_____

_____

Your answer:

_____

Evaluation questions

Objective

To understand that evaluation questions use a mix of literal, inferred and personal understanding to answer them.

Background knowledge

To answer and generate their own evaluation questions with well-reasoned responses children must understand that they need a combination of literal, inference and deduction skills – with the addition of their own understanding of the world. A variety of acceptable answers are possible because the children have to extend beyond what is given on the page to make educated guesses about events and the characters in the story.

They must first locate the literal 'who', 'what' and 'where' information within the text and pictures, then search for word and picture inference clues that suggest the characters' feelings and points of view in the story. When they add their own experience and prior knowledge to the mix it helps to guide them towards an explanation of the characters' thoughts and actions.

Skills

Explain to the children that this activity helps them to use their literal, inference and personal experiences plus evidence from the text and pictures to support their reasoning to ask and answer evaluation questions.

- **Photocopiable page 113 'Upsets and thrills'**
  - Remind the children that in order to ask and answer evaluation questions Private Detectives need to combine their literal and detective skills (see poster pages 27 'PC Page always right there!' and 63 'Being a text detective'), as well as knowledge from their own experiences, to locate word and picture clues that suggest what the characters are thinking, how they feel and why they are behaving in a particular way.

- Remind them that answers that are drawn from their own experiences also need to link to evidence in the text and pictures.
- Tell them that this activity helps them to identify feelings that are either upset or excited and asks them to locate clues and make links to ask and answer evaluation questions.
- Hand out the photocopiable sheet and talk with the children about the 'who', 'what' and 'where' information in the pictures.
- Ask them to imagine they are the people in the pictures. What do they think they are feeling from the expressions on their faces and their body language – upset or thrilled?
- Tell the children to locate the words in the captions that link to the picture clues and further explain what is happening and why.
- Ask them to generate their own questions from the information gathered following the example given on the page.

Comprehension

- **Photocopiable pages 114 and 115 'The war and Freddy'**
  - Hand out the photocopiable sheets and share the text.
  - Tell the children that to answer the questions, they need to link the clues in each question with those in the picture and text that relate to the characters' feelings. Then they should ask their own question.

Digital content

On the digital component you will find:
- Printable versions of all three photocopiable pages.
- Answers to 'The war and Freddy (2)'.
- Interactive version of 'Upsets and thrills'.

Evaluation questions

Upsets and thrills

- Look at the people in the pictures. What are they feeling and why?
- Think of some evaluation questions you could ask about the above information.

For example: *Do you think everyone was enjoying 'pass the parcel'? Why do you say that?*

Hey! The music hasn't stopped yet, Dan!

Are we nearly there? I want to get off!

Watch out!

Faster, Ben, faster!!

My new present!

Let me in!

Illustrations © 2009, Robin Edmonds/Beehive Illustration.

SCHOLASTIC
www.scholastic.co.uk **PHOTOCOPIABLE**

Evaluation questions

The war and Freddy (1)

A few months later, the war did something else. It brought Freddy's bed downstairs. It brought Mummy and Daddy downstairs as well. They slept on little camp beds in the living room with him.

The war also brought strange wailing noises outside at night.

"Sirens," said Daddy. "Air raid warnings."

It brought humming, growling noises overhead.

"The bombers are going to London," said Mummy.

The bombers went to London night after night and Freddy felt a strange excitement when he heard them.

One night, as the growly hum went on overhead, the house shook suddenly and there was a great roaring noise. Soot fell out of the chimney all over Freddy's bed.

Text © 1991, Dennis Hamley; illustration © 1991, George Buchanan.

PHOTOCOPIABLE

SCHOLASTIC
www.scholastic.co.uk

Evaluation questions

The war and Freddy (2)

1. How do you think Freddy felt when he woke up in the night? Why do you say that?

_____

_____

_____

_____

2. Do you think Freddy was frightened by the strange sounds overhead? Explain why you say that.

_____

_____

_____

_____

3. How do you think Freddy felt about the war from the clues given in the picture and text? Why do you think that?

_____

_____

_____

_____

4. Your question (Why do you think that? Why do you say that?):

_____

_____

_____

_____

Your answer:

_____

_____

_____

_____

Chapter 7

Review

Introduction

Instead of teaching children new skills, this chapter provides them with an opportunity to revise the skills they have already learned. There are two sections within the chapter. Each one provides two comprehension exercises that are levelled at a different reading age from 7–11 years, allowing you to differentiate depending on ability. For further practice, please see the 'Review' section in the Year 4 workbook.

Poster notes

Follow my leader (page 117)

All of the posters in this book could be of use in this chapter but especially poster page 117. This poster reminds the children of the process involved in exploring a piece of text fully and provides a structure that enables them to consolidate everything they have learned. Working in teams, with the teacher as score master, the children score points for each question type they ask and answer from a piece of shared text. This is a useful way for them to establish questioning and answering techniques, to identify their own comprehension strengths and weaknesses and to learn from each other.

In this chapter

	About each section	About the comprehension activity
Stories page 118	This section focuses on the revision of the skills learned in the previous chapters for reading ages 7–9.	Both are a text with illustration. One from *Toys in space* by Mini Grey and the other from *That pesky rat* by Lauren Child. Children have to use their knowledge to answer questions.
Fiction and non-fiction page 123	This section focuses on the revision of the skills learned in the previous chapters for reading ages 9–11.	One is about an African market and the other is text with illustration from *Hansel and Gretel* by Jane Ray. Children have to use their knowledge to answer questions.

Review

Follow my leader

Predicting What happens next? 	Use clues in titles, pictures, text and own experience to make predictions. Discuss predictions. Read text and show pictures.
Clarifying What does it mean? 	Identify words and phrases you do not understand. Use context clues and picture clues to work out the meaning. Ask a teacher if you cannot work out the meaning.
Questioning What questions could I ask? Score: Literal: 1 Inference: 2 Evaluation: 3 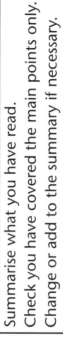	Ask questions: **who, what, where, why** and **how?** Ask and answer questions. You score points for good questions and correct answers. Discuss question type.
Retelling/summarising What have we read? 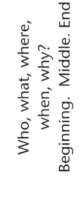Who, what, where, when, why? Beginning. Middle. End	Summarise what you have read. Check you have covered the main points only. Change or add to the summary if necessary.
Predicting Choose another leader (repeat cycle of clarifying, questioning and so on). 	Predict what you think the next sentence will be about. (Use last sentence, headings, pictures, own experiences.) Discuss predictions.

Illustrations © 2009, Robin Edmonds/Beehive Illustration.

SCHOLASTIC
www.scholastic.co.uk

PHOTOCOPIABLE

Stories

Objective

To identify the plot and sequence of events within stories and gather clues and information from the pictures and text to answer questions.

Background knowledge

These two comprehension activities are aimed at children with a reading age of 7–9 years, and focus on the skills the children have learned in the preceding chapters. They are predominantly large illustrations that carry a small amount of text, and demonstrate how pictures offer children a great stimulus for thinking on all levels.

It is important that children understand that key words in questions are linked in their meaning to clue words in the text and pictures, and that they simply need to search for similar or opposite word meanings to find the answers to the questions. These activities enable them to practice their skimming and scanning techniques to help them find the clue words in text with speed and accuracy.

Comprehension

These activities will help the children search for clues to answer literal, inference and evaluation questions from pictures and text.

● **Photocopiable pages 119 and 120 'Toys in space'**
This activity is levelled at a reading age of 7–8 years. Talk about the picture and vocabulary with the children before encouraging them to answer the literal, inference, evaluation and clarification questions from the picture and text. Each question type is awarded a mark:

- Question 1 is a literal question (1 mark)
- Question 2 is a literal question (1 mark)
- Question 3 is a clarification question (2 marks)
- Question 4 is an inference question (2 marks)
- Question 5 is an evaluation question (3 marks)

● **Photocopiable pages 121 and 122 'That pesky rat'**
This activity is levelled at a reading age of 8–9 years. Look at the picture and text with the children before they tackle the questions. Each question type is awarded a mark:

- Question 1 is a literal question (1 mark)
- Question 2 is an inference question (2 marks)
- Question 3 is an evaluation question (3 marks)
- Question 4 is an inference question (2 marks)
- Question 5 is a prediction question (2 marks)
- Question 6 is a clarification question (2 marks)

Digital content

On the digital component you will find:
● Printable versions of all four photocopiable pages.
● Answers to 'Toys in space (2)' and 'That pesky rat (2)'.
● Interactive version of 'That pesky rat'.

Name:

Stories

Toys in space (1)

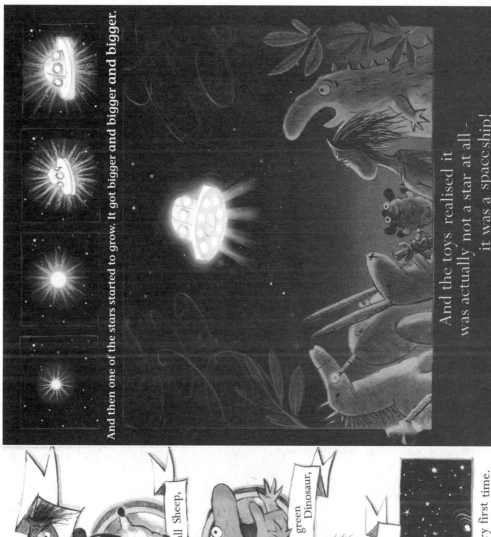

And then one of the stars started to grow. It got bigger and bigger and bigger.

And the toys realised it was actually not a star at all - it was a spaceship!

Once upon a time *(the WonderDoll said)* there were seven toys left out in the garden:

a resourceful Pink Horse,

a brave Small Sheep,

a clever Blue Rabbit,

a thoughtful green Dinosaur,

a strong little Cowboy,

a helpful wind-up Robot

and a WonderDoll.

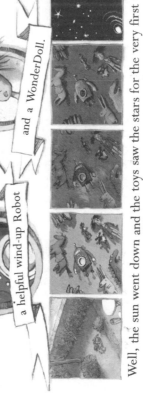

Well, the sun went down and the toys saw the stars for the very first time.

© 2012, Mini Grey.

Name:

Stories

Toys in space (2)

1. **What is this story about?**

    _____

    _____

    (1 mark)

2. **When did the toys realise that one of the stars was actually a spaceship?**

    _____

    _____

    _____

    (1 mark)

3. **The green Dinosaur is described as being 'thoughtful'. Circle the word below that has the opposite meaning to the word 'thoughtful' in the text?**

    considerate   uncaring   brainy

    (2 marks)

4. **Have the toys seen a sparkly night sky before? How do you know?**

    _____

    _____

    _____

    (2 marks)

5. **Which two toys would you take on a space adventure and why?**

    _____

    _____

    _____

    (3 marks)

PHOTOCOPIABLE   ■SCHOLASTIC
www.scholastic.co.uk

Stories

That pesky rat (1)

Text and illustrations © 2002, Lauren Child.

Name:

Stories

That pesky rat (2)

1. Who does the author describe as having 'beady eyes'?

    _____

    (1 mark)

2. Does the main character of this story live in a dirty place? How do you know that?

    _____

    _____

    (2 marks)

3. How do you think the rat feels about living where he does? Why do you say that?

    _____

    _____

    (3 marks)

4. Why do you think someone sometimes comes and empties the rat's belongings into a big van? Explain why you say that.

    _____

    _____

    (2 marks)

5. What do you predict the rat will do if they don't stop emptying his bin?

    _____

    _____

    (2 marks)

6. Explain the meaning of the word 'cutesy'.

    _____

    _____

    (2 marks)

PHOTOCOPIABLE

SCHOLASTIC
www.scholastic.co.uk

Fiction and non-fiction

Objectives

To skim and scan for literal, inferential and evaluative information. To respond to questions by locating compound words, and the same, similar or opposite meanings to key words in the questions.

Background knowledge

These two comprehension activities are aimed at children with a reading age of 9–11 years. The questions are testing the reader's understanding of vocabulary within context and also to see if the reader understands what the key words in the question actually mean.

It is important that children understand that non-fiction is about real things, people, events, and places, and fiction is story-telling about imaginary people and events that do not exist. However, even though it is concerned with facts, it does not mean that non-fiction presents only literal information. There is plenty that can be inferred or evaluated from photographs and non-fiction text – that ask for personal opinion and interpretation based on the reader's prior knowledge and experience.

Comprehension

These activities will remind the children how to understand unknown words from context and how to skim and scan for information to help them answer questions.

● **Photocopiable pages 124 and 125 'African market'**

This activity is levelled at a reading age of 9–10 years. Ask the children to search the picture and text for clues to answer literal, clarification, inference, evaluation and prediction questions. Each question type is awarded a mark:

- Question 1 is a literal question (1 mark)
- Question 2 is a clarification question (2 marks)
- Question 3 is an inference question (2 marks)
- Question 4 is an evaluation question (3 marks)
- Question 5 is a prediction question (2 marks)

● **Photocopiable pages 126 and 127 'Hansel and Gretel'**

This final comprehension activity is levelled at a reading age of 10–11 years. It asks the children to skim and scan the text for same and similar meanings to find the answers to a range of questions. Each question type is awarded a mark:

- Question 1 is a literal question (1 mark)
- Question 2 is an inference question (2 marks)
- Question 3 is a clarification question (2 marks)
- Question 4 is an inference question (2 marks)
- Question 5 is an evaluation question (3 marks)
- Question 6 is a prediction question (2 marks)

Digital content

On the digital component you will find:
- Printable versions of all four photocopiable pages.
- Answers to 'African market (2)' and 'Hansel and Gretel (2)'.
- Interactive version of 'Hansel and Gretel'.

Name:

Fiction and non-fiction

African market (1)

For hundreds of years African fabrics and clothes have been made for household and village members and for sale in the local markets. Although the earliest cloth was made mostly of local natural fibres, today's African clothing is made of a wide range of materials and in many different styles.

Photograph © Stephen Dorey / Alamy.

PHOTOCOPIABLE   ■SCHOLASTIC
www.scholastic.co.uk

Fiction and non-fiction

African market (2)

1. What has been sold in local African markets for hundreds of years?

   _____

   _____

   (1 mark)

2. Explain the meaning of 'local'.

   _____

   _____

   (2 marks)

3. Are African clothes made of a variety of materials? How do you know that?

   _____

   _____

   (2 marks)

4. Why do you think African textiles are no longer only made of local natural fibres?

   _____

   _____

   _____

   (3 marks)

5. What do you predict will be sold in the local African market of the future? Why do you say that?

   _____

   _____

   _____

   (2 marks)

Name:

Hansel and Gretel (1)

When they reached the middle of the forest, the wood-cutter helped the children to build a fire of brushwood and pine cones, and when it was burning fiercely his wife said, "Sit down beside the fire, children, and rest. We are going to chop wood. When we've done we'll come back and fetch you."

Hansel and Gretel sat together by the fire and when midday came they ate their bread. After a while they fell asleep.

When they awoke it was dark and Gretel began to cry. Hansel comforted her. "Just wait until the moon rises up and we'll soon find our way," he said. When the moon was up Hansel took his little sister by the hand and, sure enough, they found the pebbles, shining like brand new silver shillings, which showed them the way.

They walked all night long nand at daybreak reached their home. Their stepmother was furious, but their father was overjoyed, for it had cut him to the heart to leave them behind alone.

Text and illustrations © 1997, Jane Ray.

PHOTOCOPIABLE ■SCHOLASTIC
www.scholastic.co.uk

Fiction and non-fiction

Hansel and Gretel (2)

1. What did the wood-cutter's wife promise the children before she went to chop wood with her husband?

_____

_____

(1 mark)

2. What time of the day did the family reach the middle of the forest? How do you know that?

_____

_____

(2 marks)

3. Give an example of a compound word from the text. Explain what the word means.

_____

_____

_____

(2 marks)

4. Who was the elder of the two children? How do you know that?

_____

_____

(2 marks)

5. What sort of person do you think Hansel was? Explain why you say that.

_____

_____

_____

(3 marks)

6. What do you predict would have happened if it had been a rainy night? Why do you say that?

_____

_____

(2 marks)

SCHOLASTIC
ENGLISH SKILLS

Fully in line with the new curriculum objectives

Teach Key Skills in English for Years 1–6

Introducing the Scholastic English Skills series, fully matched to the new curriculum

Teacher's Books and
Pupil Workbooks in:

Handwriting

Comprehension

Spelling and vocabulary

Grammar and punctuation

Teacher's Books
Multipack savings available online

Pupil Workbooks
Multipack savings available online

Order at www.scholastic.co.uk/englishskills or call us on 0845 603 9091